Hg2 Prague

A Hedonist's guide to
Prague

BY Tremayne Carew Pole
PHOTOGRAPHY Tremayne Carew Pole

To Julia,
without whom none of
this would have been
possible.

A Hedonist's guide to Prague

Managing director – Tremayne Carew Pole
Series editor – Catherine Blake
Production – Navigator Guides
Design – P&M Design
Typesetting – Dorchester Typesetting
Repro – PDQ Digital Media Solutions Ltd
Printers – Printed in Italy by Printer Trento srl
PR – Ann Scott Associates
Publisher – Filmer Ltd
Additional photography – Andrea Plechacova

Email – info@ahedonistsguideto.com
Website – www.ahedonistsguideto.com

First Published in the United Kingdom in 2004 by
Filmer Ltd
47 Filmer Road,
London SW6 7JJ

ISBN – 0-9547878-3-8

Hg2 Prague

CONTENTS

How to…

A Hedonist's guide to… is broken down into easy to use sections: Sleep, Eat, Drink, Snack, Party, Culture, Shop, Play and Info. In each of these sections you will find detailed reviews and photographs.

At the front of the book you will find an introduction to the city and an overview map, followed by introductions to the four main areas and more detailed maps. On each of these maps you will see the places that we have reviewed, laid out by section, highlighted on the map with a symbol and a number. To find out about a particular place, simply turn to the relevant section where all entries are listed alphabetically.

Alternatively, browse through a specific section (i.e. Eat) until you find a restaurant that you like the look of. Next to your choice will be a small coloured dot – each colour refers to a particular area of the city – then simply turn to the relevant map to discover the location.

Updates

Due to the lengthy publishing process and shelf lives of books it is very difficult to keep travel guides up to date – new restaurants, bars and hotels open up all the time, while others simply fade away or just go out of style. What we can offer you are free updates– simply log onto our website www.ahedonistsguideto.com or www.hg2.net and enter your details, answer a relevant question to provide proof of purchase and you will be entitled to free updates for a year from the date that you sign up. This will enable you to have all the relevant information at your finger tips whenever you go away.

In order to help us with this any comments that you might have, or recommendations that you would like to see in the guide in future please feel free to email us at info@ahedonistsguideto.com.

The concept

A Hedonist's guide to… is designed to appeal to a more urbane and stylish traveller. The kind of traveller who is interested in gourmet food, elegant hotels and seriously chic bars – the traveller who feels the need to explore, shop and pamper themselves away from the madding crowd.

Our aim is to give you the inside knowledge of the city, to make you feel like a well-heeled, sophisticated local and to take you to the most fashionable places in town to rub shoulders with the local glitterati.

In today's world work rules our life, weekends away are few and far between, and when we do go away we want to have the most fun and relaxation possible with the minimum of stress. This guide is all about maximizing time. Everywhere is photographed, so before you go you know exactly what you are getting into; choose a restaurant or bar that suits you and your demands.

We pride ourselves on our independence and our integrity. We eat in all the restaurants, drink in all the bars and go wild in the nightclubs – all totally incognito. We charge no one for the privilege for appearing in the guide, every place is reviewed and included at our discretion.

We feel cities are best enjoyed by soaking up the atmosphere and the vibrancy; wander the streets, indulge in some retail relaxation therapy, re-energize yourself with a massage and then get ready to eat like a king and party hard in the stylish local scene.

We feel that it is important for you to explore a city on your own terms, while the places reviewed provide definitive coverage in our eyes; one's individuality can never be wholly accounted for. Whatever you do we can assure you that you will have an unforgettable weekend.

Prague

Undoubtedly one of the most beautiful cities in Europe, Prague draws in tourists from around the world to revel in its splendour. The city of a thousand spires is a stunning amalgamation of hundreds of years of architecture, from narrow, medieval streets, through Baroque, neo-Renaissance, Art Nouveau and Art Deco, culminating in cutting-edge modern design. One of the joys of visiting the city is its size – so small that all the interesting museums and churches are within walking distance of each other.

Prague is made up of many distinct districts. The heart of the city encompasses Hradčany, Mala Straná, Staré Město, Nove Město and Josefov and, as in so many other European cities, those that live in the centre tend to be the more affluent and the ex-pats. The 'real' Czechs live in surrounding areas, such as Vinohrady, ižkov and Smíchov, where the architecture may not be as beautiful and English is less widely spoken.

For the last decade Prague has become the darling of the film industry. Many films have been shot here, from *The Third Man* to more recent pictures such as *XXX* and *The League of Extraordinary Gentlemen*.

This is not just because of the architecture. To a large extent it's a result of the cost of living in the Czech Republic: workers can earn as little as a £1 an hour and a pint of beer outside the centre rarely costs more than 50p, making it an incredibly cheap place to set up a shoot.

In recent years Prague has acquired an altogether different reputation, which has come about in part because of the glut of low-cost flights. These have opened up the city, making it a centre for cheap beer and cheap sex. At weekends groups of lads in matching shirts loudly roam the streets. This guide aims to divert you away from all that and to reveal the unique attractions that Prague has to offer.

Prague's tourist industry has boomed considerably in the 15 years since the fall of Communism. At the outset there were a few hotels, a couple of traditional but mediocre restaurants and the odd grand café. Today it is a different story altogether: a multitude of eating establishments has opened up, catering to every requirement – some of them even offering gourmet food in stunning surroundings. Bars, cafés and nightclubs have developed at the same speed, and deliver the same range of sophistication.

To enjoy Prague at its finest, spend some time wandering the streets and exploring all its little nooks and crannies. Take a walk along the Royal Way from Náměstí Republiky up to the castle, relishing the sights along the way. Pop into one of the small cafés or indulge in a long, leisurely lunch on the terrace of one of the city's finest restaurants. In the evening experience a concert in one of the splendid churches or spoil yourself and take a box at the opera, followed by a gourmet dinner and a couple of cocktails. After all, the pursuit of pleasure is your ultimate goal.

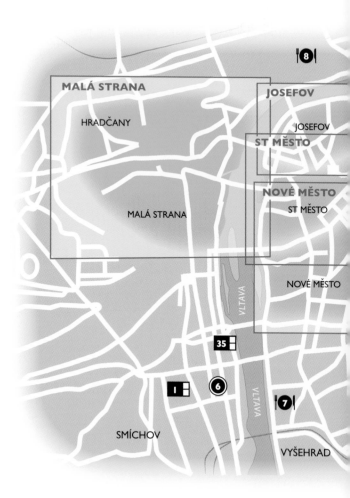

0   0.5   1 km

MALÁ STRANA

HRADČANY

JOSEFOV

JOSEFOV

ST MĚSTO

NOVÉ MĚSTO

ST MĚSTO

MALÁ STRANA

NOVÉ MĚSTO

VLTAVA

35

1   6

VLTAVA

7

SMÍCHOV

VYŠEHRAD

8

Prague   city map

DRINK

26.   Zvonarka

SLEEP

1.   Andels
25.   Le Palais
32.   Residence Belgická
35.   Riverside

SNACK

19.   Kavárna Imperial

EAT

7.   Le Bistrot de Marlène
8.   Brasserie Ullman

PARTY

1.   Akropolis
6.   Futurum
7.   Industry 55
11.   Mecca
15.   Jazz Club Zelezná
22.   K5

The Old Town

Staré Město

The Old Town is the centre of historic Prague. Tourists flock to Old Town Square to admire the scenic backdrop and gaze at the astronomical clock's hourly morality play. The narrow, cobbled streets epitomize the timelessness of the city, and lure you on to explore its secret courtyards and alleyways.

Inevitably, however, the Old Town is jammed with sightseers. The Royal Way that runs from Náměstí Republiky to Charles Bridge is often crowded with tour groups following shouty ladies with umbrellas who yell out instructions and potted histories as they go. If you want to discover the true essence of the Old Town, it's best to detach yourself from the obvious routes and attempt little detours and back routes.

While the Old Town has many excellent hotels, bars, cafés and restaurants, it is more geared towards themed and 'authentic' tourism than the rest of the city.

Owing to the narrowness of the streets and the size of the buildings, hotels in this area tend to be small and intimate. One of the best in

the city is the Hotel U Prince on Old Town Square, whose comfortable, ornate rooms and traditional elegance reflect Prague's past grandeur. The Residence Retezova is a collection of apartments in an old townhouse providing comfort and flexibility.

Many of the restaurants within the confines of the Old Town try to draw you in with 'authentic' décor, but most of these establishments are usually disappointing. However, there are some excellent finds: Flambée, a formal, designer cellar restaurant serving a French–Czech

fusion; Parnas, a glorious old-world, Art Deco, Czech restaurant with stunning views over the river and castle; and finally V Zátiší, a formal Czech–French hybrid that has been rated by some as the best in the country.

There are some notable cafés, but while it is pleasant to sit in Old Town Square and enjoy lunch basking in the sunshine, you'd be better off elsewhere. Café-Café enjoys views of the Estates Theatre, offers a great cup of coffee and plays host to the Czech *glitterati*. Nostress is a deliciously stylish café and shop hidden away behind Old Town Square; and Café Montmartre epitomizes the shabby, bohemian chic with which the locals feel so comfortable.

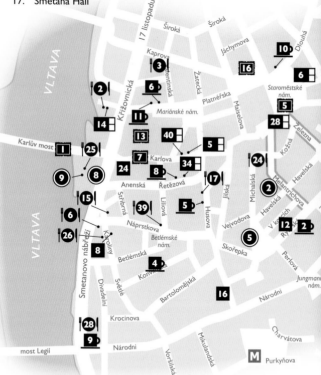

Staré Město   local map

PARTY

2. Arena
5. La Fabrique
8. Karlovy Lázně
9. Klub Lávka

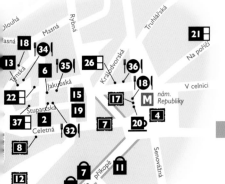

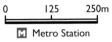

0   125   250m

M Metro Station

DRINK

2. Banana Café
6. Chateau
8. Duende
12. K.U. Café
13. Legends
15. Marquis De Sade
16. U Medvídků
18. Od Soumraku Do Úsvitu
19. Radegast
24. U Zlatého Stromu

EAT

2. Allegro
3. Arzenal
6. Bellevue
15. Don Giovanni
17. Flambée
18. Francouszka
24. U Modré Kachničky
25. Mlynec
26. Opera Grill
28. Parnas
32. La Provence
34. Rbyí Trh
35. Le Saint Jacques
36. Sarah Bernhardt
39. V Zátiší

SLEEP

5. U Červené Boty
6. Černý Slon
14. Four Seasons
21. Mercure
22. Metamorphis
26. Paříž
28. U Prince
34. Residence Řetéžová
37. Ungelt
40. U Zlaté Studny

The New Town

Nové Město

Prague's New Town is not what you might expect. Instead of concrete, glass and neon signs, there is stunning Art Nouveau and Baroque architecture. Founded in 1348 by Charles IV, the New Town has continued to grow and develop and is now in part typified by the 1920s and 1930s showpiece architecture of Wenceslas Square. Essentially an extension of the Old Town, but with wider streets, the focus is less on the tourist trade; instead this is where ordinary Czech life takes place. However, since it's still considered a chic and expensive area by the locals, the real salt-of-the-earth inhabit the districts further out, such as Zizkov, Vinohrady and beyond.

Within the New Town there are two distinct areas, separated by Wenceslas Square. To the west of this commercial centrepiece is the trendy and alternative district known as SoNa, literally 'South of the National Theatre'. Here you find Prague's designers, writers and media types, drawn to the area by the plethora of small but stylish bars and restaurants. Again these establishments fall into two categories: the simple, shabby-chic places that are old-fashioned, full of smoke and heavy cooking; and the new breed of designer cafés that serve up sushi and Californian wines.

Wenceslas Square is a dichotomy of styles: beautiful Art Nouveau edifices contrast with faceless Soviet-era, concrete department stores. This is Prague's Leicester Square, packed with tourists, large international shops and the occasional strip-joint. Commerce is definitely the name of the game, from the mainstream retail possibilities to the small-time dealers and hookers who hang around the bottom end of the square. At the top end is found the National Museum (a poor man's Natural History Museum) and the State Opera.

To the east of Wenceslas Square there is a quieter, more residential area where small shops cater to a local audience. There are also some stunning buildings, glamorous hotels and the much-vaunted Mucha museum. Na Příkopě, the shopping street that forms the border between New and Old Town, offers four or five shopping centres as well as some familiar high-street stores.

Notable restaurants in this part of town include Zahrada v Opeře, a chic and stylish establishment that is part of the State Opera complex, and Kogo, the haunt of politicians, tourists and well-placed ex-pats, while Duplex's pan-Asian cuisine is served at dizzying heights above Wenceslas Square.

This quarter is the home of the luxurious Carlo IV, arguably the Czech Republic's most opulent hotel, which contrasts dramatically with the faded, run-down glamour of the Evropa, one of Prague's oldest and most well-known establishments. There is a host of hotels dotted around the main square, but most are rather soulless and cater to tour groups and business conferences.

Nové Město is the place to go if you want to meet ordinary Czech people, not just those involved in the tourist trade, and watch them at work and play.

PARTY

3. DeMinka
4. Duplex
10. Lucerna Music Bar
12. Radost FX
14. Solidni Nejistota
17. Reduta
18. Ambassador Casino
19. Casino Palace Savarin
20. Atlas
21 Goldfingers

SHOP

4. Koruna Palace
5. Lucerna Passage
■ Jungmannova Náměstí
■ Wenceslas Square

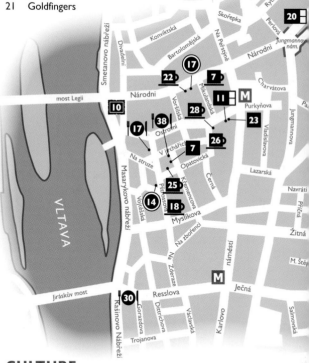

CULTURE

3. Mucha Museum
9. Wenceslas Square
10. Národní Divadlo
11. Státní Opera
18. Praha 1 & 2
19. Slovansky Dům

DRINK

7. Cheers
9. Inn Ox Bar
10. Joshua Tree
23. Ultramarin

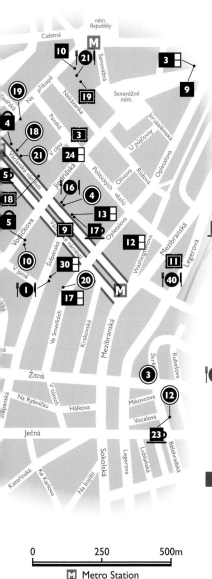

☕ SNACK

7.   Café Louvre
15. Dobrá Čajovna
17. Evropa Café
18. Globe
22. Le Patio
23. Radost FX
25. Tulip Café
26. Velryba
28. U Zlatého Soudka

🍴 EAT

1.   Alcron
16. Duplex
21. Kogo
30. La Perle de Prague
38. Universal
40. Zahrada v Opeře

▮▮ SLEEP

3.   Carlo IV
11. Elite
12. Esplanade
13. Evropa
17. K+K Hotel Fenix
20. Liberty
24. Palace
30. Radisson SAS

Josefov

The Jewish Quarter is found to the north of the Royal Way and the Old Town, but little remains of what was one of the most important Jewish communities in central Europe. It was named after Joseph II, who looked favourably on the city's Jewish community, but today tumbledown graveyards, old synagogues, narrow streets and gem dealers are all that remain of the once-proud district. Josefov is home to the original Golem, a figure of Jewish lore who used to scare children into good behaviour.

The Rudolfinium, home of the Czech Philharmonic Orchestra, presides over náměstí Jana Palacha. This open square is named after a 21-year-old who set himself alight in protest at the Soviet invasion; in a show of solidarity over 800,000 people attended his funeral. Close by stands the Museum of Decorative Arts, which displays the innovative Art Deco and Art Nouveau pieces and fine glassware for which the city is so renowned.

The sophisticated shopping street of Pařížská splits the district in two, contrasting the crumbling splendour of the Jewish community with the elegance of the modern designer retailers. This is Prague's equivalent of London's Sloane Street; international fashion houses have had a

presence here for years, and are steadily squeezing out the tackier, more tourist-orientated stores, replacing them with outlets that are more suited to the glamorous ladies who shop and lunch here.

To the east of Pařížská is where Prague's more urbane nightlife is found; the smart bars of Bugsy's, Tretters and Ocean Drive are the haunt of suited and booted businessmen and glacially cool women, who sit pouting at each other over cocktails. This is mixed with a more unconventional scene: Roxy hosts alternative bands, while students and writers swap stories in Dahab.

The streets are full of historical intrigue and the city's colourful past; narrow lanes open up onto small squares, and it is easy to lose yourself for an hour or so just wandering around and admiring the architecture and shops.

EAT

4. Barock
9. Le Café Colonial
10. Café La Veranda
14. Divini's
31. Pravda
33. Rasoi

PARTY

13. Roxy

SHOP

■ Pařížská

CULTURE

15. Rudolfinium

SLEEP

4. Casa Marcello
15. Intercontinental
16. Josef

SNACK

1. Au Gourmand
13. Dahab
16. Dolce Vita
21. Nostress Café

Štefánikův most

Ludvika Svobody nábřeží

Řásnovka

Lannova

4

Haštalská

Revoluční

Klimentská

Haštalské nám.

Hradební

Soukenická

13 13

Dlouhá

Haštalská

21

Kozí

11   4

16

Rybná

Truhlářská

Dlouhá

33

Masná

Masná

9

nám.
Republiky

Královdvorská

14   14

Týnská

Jakubská

Štupartská

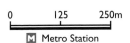

0   125   250m

M Metro Station

DRINK

1.   Alcohol Bar
4.   Bombay Cocktail Bar
5.   Bugsy's
11. Kozicka
14. MI
17. Ocean Drive
21. Tom Tom Club
22. Tretters

Hradčany/Mala Straná

Hradčany and Mala Straná are two small districts that rise up above the river to the west of Charles Bridge. Much like the rest of Prague, they are steeped in history and draw a large concentration of sight-seers determined to explore the steep, cobbled streets and feast their eyes on the fabulous architecture.

Prague's most recognizable landmark is its castle; perched above the city like a watching eagle, it has been the bastion of government for centuries. Today the castle complex has grown and expanded to become a mini-city – within its walls, churches, galleries and museums draw visitors from around the world while heads of state come to meet the government and president. This and its immediate environs make up the Hradčany district, which stretches up to the top of the hill to include the Strahov Monastery and the Loreto.

Unfortunately, apart from its cultural interest it doesn't have too much to offer the visitor. The Savoy Hotel and Domus Henrici are perched above the castle while rural U Raka lurks beneath; all three provide a good base from which to explore all the complex has to offer.

Mala Straná, like the Old Town, is packed with tourists. Forming the

western approach to Charles Bridge, the lesser quarter acts as a funnel for visitors crossing the bridge and continuing on up the Royal Way towards the castle. Consequently, on the busy Nerudova and Mostecká thoroughfares, expect to find tour groups blocking your path as they stare longingly at model houses, frightening marionettes and Prague Drinking Team T-shirts. However, it is beautiful – which is why they come flocking in droves.

Take the time to wander off the beaten track and go exploring; navigate your way round the small side streets and discover some interesting cafés or restaurants. The terrace restaurant of U Zlaté Studně hotel, for example, offers fabulous views and gourmet cuisine in serene and little travelled surroundings.

Being a distinctly touristy area, Mala Straná has a plentiful selection of hotels for you to choose from. Probably the most intriguing of these is the newly opened Aria, which is a masterpiece of ingenuity and innovation devoted to music. Likewise there are many restaurants where you can indulge your culinary fantasies. Unfortunately a number of places have recently opened to lure in sightseers tempted by the idea of 'authentic' traditional cooking; but there's little point bothering with these, when restaurants such as Kampa Park and Hergetova Cihelná can offer you excellent food in beautiful locations.

0   250   500m

M Metro Station

CULTURE

2. Kampa Museum
6. Prague Castle
7. Royal Way

SNACK

3. Café Carolina
12. Cukr Káva Limonáda
24. Sovový Mlýny
27. U Zeleného Čaje

SLEEP

2. Aria
7. Charles
8. Constans
9. Domus Balthasar
10. Domus Henrici
18. U Karlova Mostu
19. U Krále Karla
23. Neruda
27. U Páva
29. U Pštrosů
31. U Raka
33. Residence Nosticova
36. Savoy
38. Zlatá Hvězda
39. U Zlaté Studné
41. U Zlatého Kola

PARTY

16. U Malého Glena

sleep...

With the rise and fall of Communism, the Czech hotel industry has undergone many changes in the last 50 years, as borders closed and reopened again. The Velvet Revolution of 1989 caused a huge surge in tourist growth and the consequent need for accommodation. In the early 1990s a myriad of small hotels appeared in the centre, developed from grand old townhouses or by reopening and refurbishing some of the few existing hotels. During the mid-1990s established hotel brands entered the city, bringing class and convenience to tourist and business traveller alike. It is only recently that the extremely luxurious and boutique hotels have begun to appear.

Owing to the fact that many of the hotels haven't been renovated since the early 1990s, the décor and furniture have already come to look a little dated in places, with pastel carpets and bright furnishings. Others feature simpler, more traditional styles, with white walls and dark wooden furniture. Unless you book into a chain or a new boutique hotel don't expect ISDN lines and pay-per-view movies, but then there are better things to do while you're in Prague than watch films in a hotel bedroom or email your friends.

The hotels we have included in this section tend to shy away from the chain brands and lean more towards small, individual boutique hotels. Prague doesn't

have the range of extremely comfortable and luxurious small hotels that you'd find in London, Paris or New York, but there are enough to offer you a good selection.

In the last four years a range of super-chic and designer hotels has opened up in the city, filling a very obvious void in the market. Probably the most notable example of these is the Carlo IV, which opened in 2003. Owned and run by the Italian Boscolo group, it is the epitome of opulence.

All the hotels have been rated according to their style, location and atmosphere. Style takes into account the furnishings and the appearance of the hotel from inside and out. Atmosphere is based on the feel of the place: a hotel might be fantastically furnished and stylish but feel like a morgue, or it might be done up like a 1970s service station motel but still manage to create a great ambience. Location assesses how central and convenient it is for shops, restaurants and tourist attractions.

Prices quoted here are per room per night, and range from the cost of a double in low season to a suite in high season. High season runs from the beginning of April through to the end of October, and also includes Christmas and New Year.

The top 10 rated hotels in Prague are:
1. Carlo IV
2. Aria
3. Four Seasons
4. U Prince
5. Josef
6. Neruda
7. U Zlaté Studné
8. Residence Nosticova
9. U Zlatého Kola
10. Pařiz

The top five rated hotels for style are:
1. Carlo IV
2. Aria
3. U Prince
4. Josef
5. Residence Nosticova

The top five rated hotels for location are:
1. Four Seasons
2. U Prince
3. Evropa
4. Residence Retezova
5. Černý Slon

The top five rated hotels for atmosphere are:
1. Aria
2. Neruda
3. U Zlaté Studné
4. Carlo IV
5. Josef

Andels, Stroupežnického 21, P5.
Tel: 296 889 688 www.andelshotel.com
Rates: 7,440–10,230kc

Along with the Josef, this is Prague's answer to the design hotel
revolution. Designed by Jestico + Whiles, the force behind
London's The Hempel and One Aldwych, Andels was commis-
sioned by the Vienna International group – owners of the Palace,
Le Palais and the Savoy. Part of Smichov's commercial centre, the
hotel has 231 rooms, which primarily accommodate business
clientele, since it's close to the Convention Centre and can host
conferences. This shouldn't deter the leisure traveller, however,
especially as very favourable weekend rates can be negotiated. Its
strikingly modern interior is a mixture of functionality and innovative design. Rooms are equipped with DVD players and ISDN
lines while the bathrooms use glass and contemporary appli-
ances. A trendy bar and a good restaurant are necessary as the
surrounding area isn't overly salubrious and there are few decent
eating establishments.

Style 8/9, Atmosphere 7/8, Location 7

Aria, Tržiště 9, P1.
Tel: 225 334 111 www.ariahotel.net
Rates: 10,075–30,225kc

31

Definitely one of Prague's best hotels, the Aria was opened in September 2003. It's tucked in beside the American embassy, which is perhaps not the safest place to be, but it's certainly worth the risk. The Aria is a musically themed hotel, with all 52 rooms decorated to represent a different musical style, from Rossini to reggae, and from Brahms to Celtic New Age. Each room and public area has been painstakingly styled by Italian designer Rocco Magnoli, who counts Versace amongst his clients. The bedrooms also boast flat-screen computers, DVD players and Molton Brown bath products, and they're large, the beds huge and the taste exquisite. The bar and breakfast areas are equally elegant and each evening a film with a musical theme is shown in the comfortable cinema. There's also the option of locking yourself in the private screening room with a couple of friends and a bottle of wine, and watching a film. This is accommodation of the highest quality, beguilingly beautiful, charming and well thought out. If you can't afford to stay here, at least pop in for a drink on a sunny day and admire the stunning roof terrace views.

Style 9/10, Atmosphere 9, Location 8/9

Carlo IV, Senovážné Náměstí 13, P1.
Tel: 224 593 090 www.boscolohotels.com
Rates: 8,050–32,100kc

Opulent would be an understatement for the newest Boscolo

offering in Prague – it is beyond indulgent. The Carlo IV opened in 2003 after a three-year and multi-million pound redevelopment. It was formerly Prague's main post office and a bank, and many of the original features are noticeable as soon as you walk up the main entrance steps. The reception is absolutely stunning

– a vast rectangular space where the tellers would have dealt with customers. A long, stylish bar, fabulous restaurant and a modish health club are just some of the features on offer, along with a small cigar bar housed in what would once have been the bank vault, with the original safe doors still in place and valuables replaced by bottles of wine. The 152 rooms are elegantly and tastefully decorated, fusing comfort and style with modern simplicity. This is undoubtedly the chicest hotel in Prague and still relatively quiet.

Style 9/10, Atmosphere 8/9, Location 9

Casa Marcello, Řásnovka 783, P1.
Tel: 222 310 260 www.casa-marcello.cz
Rates: 4,350–5,900kc

Set in a picturesque townhouse next to the St Agnes monastery, this small boutique hotel attracts a refined and elegant clientele. It has the aristocratic feel of an old palace, furnished with assorted antiques and pictures. Casa Marcello is located just off an old cobbled square in Josefov, close to the centre of the nightlife and

33

not far from Old Town Square, yet it still manages to retain a sense of tranquillity. Attached to the hotel are the highly reputed restaurant Agnes and a terrace restaurant in the courtyard that acts as a summer suntrap and a peaceful breakfast area. Although

some of the rooms feel a little anonymous and don't exude as much character as the rest of the building, they are still comfortable, clean and quiet.

Style 7, Atmosphere 8, Location 8/9

Černý Slon, Týnská 1, P1.

Tel: 222 321 521 www.hotelcernyslon.cz
Rates: 3,100–5,400kc

A small boutique hotel backing on to the Týn Church just yards from Old Town Square. The 13 rooms have just 35 beds; all are

furnished in a traditional manner, and are clean and simple. The townhouse, which accommodates the hotel, dates back to the 14th century and has been comprehensively renovated in the last couple of years. The atmosphere generated by the staff and owners is very friendly and laid-back: nothing happens in a hurry. There is a decent restaurant, café and wine bar attached, a welcome and convenient option for the exhausted tourist. Its appeal lies in its superb location, simple, quiet rooms and friendly atmosphere.

Style 7/8, Atmosphere 8, Location 9

U Červené Boty, Karlova 5, P1.
Tel: 222 221 051
Rates: 3,900–5,300kc

A tiny boutique 'pension' offering only four suites and located slap bang on the Royal Way, running from Old Town Square to the castle. Built in the 17th century and renovated as a hotel in 1996, it offers bedrooms that are all furnished with antique furniture and heavy wooden beds, while the bathrooms are fresh, clean and bright. The owners have done as much as they can to preserve the original features and feel of the building. The suites are spacious and reasonably bright, but those overlooking the street tend to get noisy quite early in the morning, with the thronging of the tourist horde. A great little place to stay, very central and with much of its original charm. Good value for what

and where it is.

Charles, Josefská 1, P1.
Tel: 257 532 913 www.selectmarketinghotels.com
Rates: 4,350–12,400kc

The Charles hotel sits about 100 yards from its eponymous
bridge. The 22 rooms and nine suites are all furnished with
antique wooden wardrobes and beds; retaining their original
wooden ceilings, they are spacious, and have proved a popular
choice. The hotel is elegant and in keeping with the architecture
of the area. It might not be as state of the art as other hotels,
but it gives you a warm welcome, is perfectly situated and oozes
authentic character and charm. It does get very busy at weekends so you will be unlikely to pick up a last-minute reservation.
One of the most authentic hotels in the centre of Prague.

Style 8, Atmosphere 8, Location 9

Constans, Břetislavova 309, P1.
Tel: 234 091 818 www.hotelconstans.cz
Rates: 4,530–7,300kc

Opened in 2002, this little boutique hotel with 32 rooms is to be found in a side street just beneath the castle. Constans is a more up-market sibling of the Metamorphis Hotel on Tyn; its 16th-century building has been restored and decorated in a characteristically Czech way, with heavy wooden furniture and plain white walls. Many original features have been retained and the rooms are bright and comfortable, if slightly spartan. A small breakfast area and a basic international restaurant just off the lobby serve decent food. Constans is a relaxing and traditional hotel in a quiet location, though it is quite easy to get disorientated in the surrounding streets.

Style 8, Atmosphere 7/8, Location 7/8

Domus Balthasar, Mostecká 5, P1.
Tel: 257 199 499 www.domus-balthasar.cz
Rates: 3,040–6,400kc

The younger sibling of the Hidden Places duo in Prague, Balthasar has a more stylish, design-led approach to accommodation than its brother Henrici. The eight rooms have been decorated with a modern, fresh eye; simple white walls and linen contrast with dark wooden furniture and simple pine floors, and each room is equipped with state-of-the-art televisions and DVD. The down-side to the hotel is that it has no public spaces so you can only spend time in your room – it's purely a place to stay, while a café around the corner serves breakfast. The hotel opened late in 2003 and is found a few steps from Charles

Bridge; if you book into one of the corner deluxe doubles you can enjoy interesting views towards the bridge and its flanking tower.

Style 8, Atmosphere 7/8, Location 8/9

Domus Henrici, Loretánská 11, P1.
Tel: 220 511 369 www.domus-henrici.cz
Rates: 3,040–6,400kc

Close to Prague Castle, this quiet backstreet residence has eight double rooms set in a charming period house. The rooms and terraces have panoramic views over the city and the beautiful Petrin gardens below. Simply furnished, the rooms manage to preserve all the comforts that one might expect from a modern

hotel, while remaining spacious and light. The area, although central, is close to the top of Castle Hill, which means a tiring walk home at the end of the day… but then again, that's why God invented taxis. The energetic will be amply rewarded, however: this is an incredibly beautiful, unspoilt part of town brimming with historical buildings and character.

Style 7/8, Atmosphere 7/8, Location 7

Elite, Ostrovni 32, P1.
Tel: 224 932 250 www.hotelelite.cz
Rates: 3,800–6,500kc

One of the few hotels in the trendy SoNa area of Prague, renovated and reopened in 2000, although the original building dates back to the 14th century. Today it is a comfortable and charming place in a lively and interesting part of town, which doesn't quite follow the SoNa accent of modern, contemporary and designer; instead it has created an entity that is comfortable and traditional. The hotel retains many of its original features: murals on the ceilings, ornate stuccowork and simple beams. The Elite is kitted out with heavy wooden furniture which works well with the modern hotel facilities. On the ground floor are a lively bar and nightclub that are definitely worth a visit, accessed from the street through a separate entrance. A courtyard provides a great summer breakfast area as well as an ambient, tranquil location for a quiet evening drink.

Esplanade, Washingtova 19, P1.
Tel: 224 501 111 www.esplanade.cz
Rates: 3,069–12,369kc

Esplanade is a large and attractive Art Nouveau hotel at the southern end of Wenceslas Square, close to the State Opera. Opened in 1927, it has 74 elegant and comfortable rooms, filled with reproduction antique furniture. Grand in appearance, the hotel manages to retain an individual touch, with most rooms individually furnished along Art Nouveau lines. A smart lobby café and decent restaurant are reminiscent of the old-world splendour so typical of Prague. The hotel has sizeable conference facilities, which might mean you share your romantic weekend away with 40 Japanese businessmen. The Esplanade is well located for opera buffs who fancy a couple of evenings indulging their passion at the opera house across the road. Comfortable and stylish.

Evropa, Václavské náměstí 25, P1.
Tel: 224 228 117 www.evropahotel.cz
Rates: 1,430–4,000kc

Prague's bastion of faded grandeur, this quintessentially Art

Nouveau building on Wenceslas Square was once *the* hotel to stay in. Today it is a rather shabby monument to past glories, frequented by those in search of a truly pre-Communist experience. The 90 rooms and three suites seem to be stuck in a time warp: tattered Louis XVI furniture, ornate stucco and threadbare carpets abound. The communal, internal spaces are magnificent examples of Art Nouveau swagger, with fantastic chandeliers and swirling lines. The hotel has two restaurants and a café all in the same style, which overcharge tourists looking for that *bona fide olde* Prague experience amid the modern monstrosities of the large square. The rates, on the other hand, are very reasonable, but don't expect many luxuries. This is the place to come and relive history, to imagine what once was and no longer is.

Style 8/9, Atmosphere 7, Location 9

Four Seasons, Veleslavínova 2a, P1.
Tel: 221 427 000 www.fourseasons.com
Rates: 8,680–68,200kc

Having opened early in 2001, almost immediately the Four Seasons was forced to close for a year after the 2002 floods, but has reopened as luxurious as ever. The 162 rooms and suites display all the extravagance that you have come to expect from this exclusive brand. Its USP is its unbeatable location on the river bank with fantastic views rising towards the castle and over

Charles Bridge. One of the highlights of a stay here is taking in dinner on a balmy summer's evening on the terrace of the Allegro restaurant. The rooms are kitted out with all the luxury and mod-cons that you could hope for – but it is just this level of service and attention that makes the Four Seasons slightly predictable. You will meet the same clientele time and time again around the world, whichever member of the group you stay in. But this is still a fantastic hotel and definitely one of the best that Prague has to offer.

Style 8/9, Atmosphere 8, Location 9/10

Intercontinental, Náměstí Curieovych 5, P1.
Tel: 296 631 111 www.prague.intercontinental.com
Rates: 8,370–12,100kc

This was the first Intercontinental to arrive in Prague, built in the 1970s during the period of Soviet Occupation. The hotel was damaged badly in the 2002 floods and had to close for a three-month period while it was refurbished. Today its position at the top of fashionable Pařížská means that it attracts the affluent for its proximity to some of Prague's most stylish boutiques and chic restaurants. The hotel comes equipped with all the conveniences that you could possibly need, including a state-of-the-art fitness centre that boasts an impressive golf simulator on which execs can play the Belfry or Augusta in between conferences. On the roof, the Zlatá Praha restaurant gives guests a scenic dining experience with views of many of Prague's thousand spires. While stylish and well equipped, the Intercontinental has not yet managed to create its own personality, but instead relies on the branding opportunities that the hotel group affords.

Style 8, Atmosphere 8, Location 8/9

Josef, Rybná 20, P1.
Tel: 221 700 111 www.hoteljosef.com
Rates: 5,344–9,472kc

A member of the Design Hotels group, this is the first hotel of its kind to open up in the Czech Republic. Josef was designed by Eva Jiricna, a Czech architect working in London with a reputation for creating uniquely modern interiors. It is probably the most contemporary and modern of the hotels in Prague, minimal in concept yet elegant in feel. The hotel is situated close to Old Town Square amid the hubbub of bars and restaurants. Located on a quiet street, however, inside a rather bland modern building, Hotel Josef has a sleek and ultra-fashionable interior. A large modern bar and café make a stylish location for a mid-morning coffee or early evening cocktails. The rooms are incredibly comfortable, with a whole host of mod-cons (internet connection, DVD player, etc.), while the executive rooms are fabulously spacious, with a glass bathroom wall. The staff go out of their way to ensure that the guests have everything they need. There is a rooftop bar and fitness centre where you can relax and work

43

out while admiring the view over the city.

Style 9, Atmosphere 8/9, Location 8/9

K + K Hotel Fenix, Ve Smečkách 30, P1.
Tel: 233 092 222 www.kkhotels.com
Rates: 8,250kc

An elegant hotel on a side street running off Wenceslas Square.
Despite being part of the K + K Hotel chain, Fenix is remarkably
stylish and contemporary. A light, open and airy lobby creates a
great first impression and doesn't flatter to deceive. The hotel
caters to a young crowd, and features a combination of sharp
interior design and state-of-the-art amenities. This is a big hotel,
and the 130 rooms are simply and gracefully decorated with
muted colours and modern furniture. There is a health club in

the basement and a business centre just off the lobby. The neighbourhood might appear a little dog-eared (with a couple of
'nightclubs' close by), but it is in the centre of town with most of
the cultural and entertainment hotspots just a short walk away.
As with many of the larger hotels it tends to attract business
travellers, but it does make an excellent central base for tourists
as well.

Style 7/8, Atmosphere 8, Location 7/8

U Karlova Mostu, Na Kampá 15, P1.
Tel: 257 531 430 www.archibald.cz
Rates: 3,800–7,000kc

No further than a small child can throw from its eponymous
bridge, U Karlova Mostu has risen from the flood-damaged Na
Kampe 15. The 26 rooms and suites are spread over three
floors, with the best rooms on the top floor (especially No. 24,
and at no extra cost). Inside, U Karlova Mostu's design is typically Czech – white walls, wooden floors, low ceilings and heavy
wooden furniture. The problem is the lack of sophistication, sac-
rificed for 'authentic' tourist charm, but what it lacks in style is
more than compensated for in location and price – half of the
rooms overlook the river and the glorious frontage of the Old
Town. Two pubs beneath the hotel will always ensure that it's a
lively destination, if not packed exclusively with tourists, especially on a warm summer's day when you can sit on the river bank

clutching a glass of cool Czech beer.

> **Style 8, Atmosphere 7/8, Location 7/8**

● **U Krále Karla, Úvoz 4, P1.**
Tel: 257 531 211 www.romantichotels.cz
Rates: 3,900–7,900kc

The sister hotel to the U Páva, but set further up the hill towards the castle, U Karla is part of the Romantic Hotels chain. The rooms are sumptuously adorned with period furniture, and many of the original features remain, including painted ceilings and stained-glass windows. There are 16 rooms and three suites in this Gothic building, which was rebuilt in 1639 into a Baroque house. A small, intimate and low-lit restaurant next to the reception has a good wine list for a romantic dinner. U Karla is in a great location with enough good restaurants and cafés nearby to make it a viable place to be, but it could be a little far up the hill for some.

> **Style 7, Atmosphere 7/8, Location 9**

● **Liberty, 28 října 11, P1.**
Tel: 224 239 598 www.hotelliberty.cz
Rates: 4,800–7,300kc

Set just off Wenceslas Square on a busy pedestrian shopping street, this small hotel has 32 rooms and suites. The rooms are, sadly, decorated in a faux-antique manner and lack character. But it does have all the facilities a modern traveller would expect, and the energetic visitor might enjoy the fitness centre in the basement,

equipped with exercise machines, a sauna and a whirlpool bath. The small breakfast room and a large outdoor terrace for the summer provide decent eating areas. Ask for a room on the upper floors to take advantage of the views of the castle. The hotel is always busy because of its very central location, so be prepared to put up with the noise, hustle and bustle, and plentiful offers from the ladies of the night who hang out just around the corner.

Style 7, Atmosphere 7/8, Location 9

Mercure, Na Poříčí 7, P1.
Tel: 221 800 800 www.mercure.com
Rates: 4,000–6,800kc

Despite being part of a French hotel chain, the Mercure is highly individual, smart and modern. The building underwent an extensive refurbishment in 2001/02, transforming it from its previous incarnation as the home of an insurance company where Franz Kafka, poet, writer and hero of angst-ridden teenagers, was reputed to have worked for 14 years. Many original features are retained: high doors open into the elegant bedrooms, and the

47

suite built into the tower offers spectacular views over the rooftops and the city panorama. There's a relaxing Library Bar, styled like an old English gentleman's club with the requisite deep, leather armchairs and books; meanwhile, the restaurant specializes in steak tartare in a variety of different forms, to be washed down with great local and French wine. With accommodating and friendly service, this is a great place to enjoy all the comforts of a chain hotel without too much of the anonymity.

Style 8/9, Atmosphere 8, Location 7/8

Metamorphis, Malá Štupartská 5, P1.
Tel: 221 771 011 www.metamorphis.cz
Rates: 4,530–7,300kc

This pleasant and airy hotel hides behind a dreary pavement café and an unwelcoming, bland reception. The rooms are clustered around a quiet, enclosed courtyard tucked away to the rear of the building; they are large, light and airy, with enormous pieces of dark, heavy furniture. Original chandeliers droop from the ceilings and heels click imperiously on wooden floors, but the furnishings look as though they were chosen by a colour-blind interior decorator. Metamorphis is very central, sitting in a fashionable little square just behind Old Town Square; there is a reasonable restaurant in the basement, but don't bother with the ground-floor terraced café. If you're looking for rest, aim for the top two floors, since there is a lively bar just around the corner that can get a little noisy at night.

Style 6/7, Atmosphere 7, Location 9

Neruda, Nerudova 44, P1.
Tel: 257 535 557 www.hotelneruda-praha.cz
Rates: 5,760–7,050kc

One of our favourites, set just beneath the castle on the busy Nerudova tourist route, which now ranks among the most stylish hotels in the city. The original building dates from the 14th century, and it retains its simple but beautiful façade and presence. Recently renovated, it has become an island of tranquillity and design. The entrance lobby, café and lounge on the ground floor set the tone: clean lines, simple materials and designer furniture, which become familiar motifs. The 20 rooms are elegant,

painted in neutral colours with simple white bed linen, while the bathrooms are light and modern, all equipped with the facilities expected of a first-rate hotel. The Neruda is a shining example of how old and new can be combined successfully, and seems wonderfully uncluttered and spacious. Definitely one of our favourites – and it does mean a hot chocolate!

Style 8/9, Atmosphere 9, Location 8

● **Palace, Panská 12, P1.**
Tel: 224 093 111 www.palacehotel.cz
Rates: 4,000–10,750kc

One of the smartest hotels in Prague, the Palace is right in the centre of town. Aptly named, it was first opened in 1909, and in its current incarnation it is part of the Vienna International Hotels group. Offering exactly what you would expect from an old-world hotel, there are signs of continuing grandeur everywhere, most notably in the lobby and the façade of the hotel. There is a good restaurant and a decent bar attached. If you need anything organized the concierge service will go out of its way to accommodate. The one-time glory of the rooms may have faded somewhat, but has been replaced by comfortable and functional furnishings. The hotel is popular with high-class tour groups and conferences, but it still retains an up-market and individual feel. Good if you want that sense of security that a chain hotel sometimes brings.

Style 8/9, Atmosphere 8, Location 8/9

Le Palais, U Zvonarky 1, P1.
Tel: 222 563 351 www.palaishotel.cz
Rates: 5,720–51,200kc

This edifice was constructed in the mid 19th-century and entirely renovated in 2001/02 by the Vienna International Hotels
group. Located, unsurprisingly, in what was once a palace, this
beautiful building still retains many of its original features, wood-
en ceilings, stuccowork and murals. The modern hotel is
equipped with all the necessary mod-cons, a great restaurant,
relaxing bar and one of the few health spas in Prague. Le Palais is
a beautiful place to stay, although it is located perhaps a 30-
minute walk (or a 10-minute taxi ride) from the centre. But if
you want to explore a separate, pleasant corner of town, the
Vinohrady neighbourhood is quiet and affluent, and there are a
few interesting bars and restaurants in the area. The 64 rooms
are comfortable, if tainted with the slightly predictable chain-
hotel furniture and coverings. It is worth paying the extra for
one of the suites with an open fireplace – they certainly add to
the romance of this grand old dame.

Style 8/9, Atmosphere 7/8, Location 5

Paříz, U Obecního domu 1, P1.
Tel: 222 195 195 www.hotel-pariz.cz
Rates: 10,240–41,600kc

A classic Art Nouveau hotel in the centre of Prague, Paříz is probably the most up-market in town. Built in 1904 next to the Municipal House, another grand Art Nouveau edifice, the hotel retains its turn-of-the-century elegance even though subsequent renovations have modernized it. The rooms are comfortable and incorporate new furniture designed with an Art Nouveau twist, but the soft furnishings and carpets were more anonymous than we would have hoped for. They all have large double doors opening off the corridor; the bathrooms are clean, crisp and covered in French cobalt and white tiles. If you can afford to splash out, the Royal Tower Suite is extremely luxurious. Planned like a loft apartment with sympathetically designed furniture, it is capped by fabulous 360° views of the city. The restaurant, bar and lobby all show evidence of resplendent grandeur, and the hotel has all the facilities that you might expect or need, including a small fitness centre and sauna. The restaurant, Sarah Bernhardt, is fantastic, the food sumptuous; and the café is a great place for a spot of afternoon tea – but of course, you will pay for it all handsomely.

Style 8/9, Atmosphere 8, Location 8/9

U Páva, U Lužického semináře, P1.
Tel: 257 533 573 www.romantichotels.cz
Rates: 4,500–7,900kc

U Páva, meaning the 'At the Peacock', was one of the first hotels
to be renovated after the Velvet Revolution, saving the house
from destruction and retaining much of its historical character. It
now offers 19 rooms and eight suites, scattered among1 its three
buildings. It's certainly one of the most romantic hotels in the city,
with some of the rooms having views up towards the castle.
Plentiful wooden panelling, painted wooden ceilings, rich textiles
and ornate period furniture all set the scene. A stylish restaurant
and café are attached to the hotel, with large leather armchairs
to sink into. One of the most traditional and comfortable hotels
in the city, U Páva is ideal for a romantic weekend away, particularly in winter. It enjoys a location on a quiet street not far from
the river, a couple of minutes from Charles Bridge.

Style 8/9, Atmosphere 8, Location 8/9

U Prince, Staromžstské náměstí 29, P1.
Tel: 224 213 807 www.hoteluprince.cz
Rates: 4,190–10,990kc

This is one of the more original and romantic hotels in the city,
constructed in the shell of a 12th-century building. You couldn't

ask for a more central location, on Old Town Square itself, just a few steps from the astronomical clock. The 15 rooms, seven suites and two apartments are all furnished with heavy antique wooden furniture and tasteful decorations, and the original wooden ceilings have been restored to their painted splendour. Having undergone a major refurbishment in 2001, the hotel is now equipped with a smartly arranged terrace on the square, a seafood restaurant, a wine bar and a stunning roof terrace with fantastic views out over the city. U Prince maintains its intimacy and emphasizes tranquillity and service. For a piece of the past and an almost unsurpassed feeling of romance in the city, this is the place to stay, but you do pay the price.

Style 9, Atmosphere 8/9, Location 9/10

U Pštrosů, Náměstí Dražického 12, P1.
Tel: 257 532 410 www.upstrosu.cz
Rates: 5,300–15,000kc

Located literally on one end of Charles Bridge, 'The Three Ostriches' is one of Prague's most blatantly tourist-focused hotels, and you will pay for the privilege of staying here. There are some fantastic suites, which overlook the bridge towards the river. While this may sound amazing, remember Prague's nightlife goes on until the early hours and the bridge is popular 24 hours a day, as a route home or a wooing spot for young lovers, so it can be noisy. The rooms to the rear are quieter, but not desperately inspiring, nor in the same league as the suites. A decent restaurant lurks beneath the hotel, and the staff are friendly. Most rooms retain their historical character, furnished with a mixture of old and new, combining comfort with tradition. A good place to stay if you want to be in the heart of everything.

Style 7, Atmosphere 8, Location 9

Radisson SAS Alcron, Štěpánská 40, P1.
Tel: 222 820 000 www.radissonsas.com
Rates: 7,100–11,300kc

While we may be disinclined to rave about chain hotels, this really is something a little more special. Before the Radisson group took it over, the Alcron hotel was a Prague institution for many years. It displays a strong Art Deco influence and retains many of the original features – heavy crystal chandeliers, rich Italian marble and creamy 'milk glass' – enough to drive home the feeling that you couldn't be anywhere else in the world other than Prague. The 211 rooms are very comfortable and designed to complement the communal areas with classic period furnishings. The clientele comprise business travellers and affluent tour groups. Its central location, just off Wenceslas Square and a 10-minute stroll from Old Town Square, puts you close to the opera houses. The Alcron restaurant is one of the finest in the city, specializing entirely in seafood, while La Rotonde is an Art Deco marvel and produces excellent meat dishes. Worth it for the food alone.

Style 8, Atmosphere 7/8, Location 8

● **U Raka, Černínská 10, P1.**
Tel: 220 511 10 www.romantikhotels.com/prag
Rates: 6,200–7,900kc

Hidden away in a beautiful, unspoilt part of the city is this small, romantic hotel, designed to look like a country farmstead with wooden timbers, trickling water, greenery and various agricultural knick-knacks. It is an oasis of tranquillity, since there is very little here to distract you. The rooms are furnished in an elegant but basic manner, with wrought-iron or heavy wooden beds and

farmhouse furniture with muted plain colours. Natural materials abound and provide a return to nature, heightened by the small and sensitively landscaped garden areas. Beware the location, which means a longish walk to Old Town Square and Staré Město, but it also means a peaceful stay.

Style 8, Atmosphere 8, Location 6

Residence Belgická, Belgická 12, P2.
Tel: 221 401 800 www.mamaisonresidences.com
Rates: 4,000–9,280kc

For a totally different kind of place to stay, try these serviced apartments. They cater primarily for business travellers, but are often available at the weekends or for a couple of days during the week. The owners provide an excellent concierge service delivering food, drink and whatever else you desire. They opened in 2002 with 30 fully loaded units of modern design, kitted out in a contemporary and sophisticated style. There is a large outdoor garden terrace and spacious common areas. If you can get a reservation, these apartments are great, if slightly far out of the centre – 30 minutes to walk in or 5 to drive – but there are some decent bars and restaurants in the neighbourhood. Good if you want a quiet weekend away from everything in a genuine Czech neighbourhood, with few tourists and a sense of adventure.

Style 8/9, Atmosphere 8, Location 5

Residence Nosticova, Nosticova 1, P1.
Tel: 257 312 513 www.nosticova.com
Rates: 5,000–16,500kc

A firm favourite with Prague's film industry, this 10-room hotel often becomes home to visiting actors and directors for the duration of their shoot. Each of the suites is traditionally furnished, but unlike other 'traditional' establishments, these are tasteful. One of the most interesting suites is the Arcimboldo, which houses the hotel's only four-poster and therefore becomes the romantic room of choice. Although the accommodation lacks the mod-cons that most other high-end hotels offer, the emphasis is on service and relaxation. Residence Nosticova is delightfully tranquil, tucked away on a small side street to the side of Charles Bridge. On the ground floor is the newly refurbished Alchemy restaurant, providing succour for those simply too tired or relaxed to venture out for the evening.

Style 8/9, Atmosphere 8, Location 8

Residence Řetězová, Řetězová 9, P1.
Tel: 222 221 800 www.residenceretezova.cz
Rates: 3,840–12,000kc

Like the Belgická above, this is a collection of nine serviced apartments set in a townhouse, but much more central. Situated close to the Royal Way, they range in size from a small studio to large two-bedroom flats. All are furnished in a different style and titled with the names of European capital cities, but without any obvious similarities to their namesakes. Many original features are still in place, with vaulted ceilings and frescoed wooden panelling, while some preserve the original 15th-century roof frames. They each have a small kitchen with state-of-the-art cooking facilities. Again, a concierge service provides you with any meals you need, as well as concert bookings, car hire arrangements and even baby-sitting. Breakfast is not included but there are three very good cafés within 20 yards of the front door. An interesting place to stay, especially good for a youngish family, with a great location and friendly staff.

Style 8, Atmosphere 8, Location 9

Riverside, Janáčkovo Nábřeží 15, P5.
Tel: 225 994 611 www.riversideprague.com
Rates: 7,040–18,880kc

The Riverside opened in 2002 and has made inroads into Prague's designer hotel scene. A product of the French group Orco, also responsible for Residence Belgická, the hotel combines modern elegance and comfort with old-fashioned style and breathtaking views. Situated on the river bank, as the name suggests, Riverside overlooks not just the river but the castle as well – and Frank Gehry's impressive Dancing House. Simple but stylish rooms are the product of Pascale de Montrémy's design vision, and include the comfortable Room 603 which has a stunning panorama and balcony. A relaxed and modish lobby bar is the perfect place to sip a cocktail while you wait for your partner to get ready. However, as it's just on the other side of Jiráskuv Most, it does mean that it is a brisk 10-minute walk into the centre.

Style 8/9, Atmosphere 8, Location 7

Savoy, Keplerova ul. 6, P1.
Tel: 224 302 430 www.hotel-savoy.cz
Rates: 10,240–31,680kc

One of the old guard in terms of hotel names, this 55-room establishment is one of the more popular with the A-list, and often plays host to visiting football teams because of its location close to the training pitches. The hotel was reopened in 1994, retaining its original façade and many of its original features. Internally it is what one might expect from a Savoy, stuffed full of marble, modern amenities and predictably patterned carpets. A restaurant serves excellent international and Czech food, however the hotel tends to be full of those people who rely on the brand to be comfortable, luxurious and sophisticated, hence the atmosphere can be slightly rarefied at times. The service is excellent and the staff incredibly friendly but nevertheless the hotel lacks an air of romance. Located at the top of the castle hill, there are plenty of neighbouring attractions and a few restaurants but it lacks the vibrancy associated with Old Town Square and its surrounds.

Style 8, Atmosphere 7/8, Location 7

Ungelt, Malá Štupartská 1, P1.
Tel: 224 828 686 www.ungelt.cz
Rates: 4,500–6,800kc

Located close to Old Town Square, this small boutique hotel offers a miniature snapshot time capsule, with different parts of the hotel dating back through various reconstructions to the 12th century. The 10 apartments are split into either one or two bedrooms, characterfully furnished with a mixture of antique furniture and 1990s Eastern European flair. Each has its own kitchen and dining facilities, with breakfast delivered to the room each

morning. The name 'Ungelt' is derived from the tariff that the merchants would pay to bring their goods into the city. The only minus is the proximity to one of Prague's livelier American college bars, so if your room is on the east side of the building it can be quite noisy. For a small hotel they haven't scrimped on space; the suites are large and for the most part quiet, and give you a real sense of independence from the traditional hotel format.

Style 7/8, Atmosphere 7, Location 9

Zlatá Hvězda, Nerudova 48, P1.
Tel: 257 532 867 www.hotelgoldenstar.com
Rates: 3,648–7,232kc

The Golden Star Hotel, an imposing building with 24 rooms and two apartments, sits at the top of Nerudova on the way up to the castle. In the 14th century it belonged to the mayor of Prague, and after going through through many private ownerships it reopened to the public in May 2000. Original architectural features remain and the reconstruction has highlighted many of the key aspects while managing to incorporate a modern standard of comfort. The rooms are very comfortable and the reproduction antique furniture combines well with the architecture in its simplicity; wooden floors and light walls pervade. A sizeable restaurant on the ground floor with a terrace on the street affords views down the touristy but picturesque road. It is

a beautiful hotel but perhaps too far up the hill for some, and the better nightlife and restaurants are on the far side of the river. Good for a little romance.

Style 8, Atmosphere 8, Location 8

U Zlaté Studně, U Zlaté Studně 4, P1.
Tel: 257 533 322 www.uzlatestudne.cz
Rates: 5,150–9,900kc

A fantastic hotel set beneath the castle walls and a stone's throw from the British Embassy. The 16th-century Renaissance building that houses it was renovated to create 17 rooms and three suites. All have been done up to a high standard, using reproduction furniture from the 17th, 18th and 19th centuries. Each room contains a whirlpool bath and heated bathroom floors but it is the spectacular views, looking out over most of the Old Town, stretching away up to Žižkov and beyond, that you are paying for. There is a restaurant on the top floor with an outside terrace which enjoys the most fantastic panorama as well as serving top class food. Not only is it central but it is quiet as well, set at the end of a small alley so there is no surrounding traffic. Your only distraction comes from the tinkle of running water from the hotel's gardens below.

Style 8/9, Atmosphere 8/9, Location 8/9

U Zlaté Studny, Karlova 3, P1.

Tel: 222 220 130 www.uzlatestudny.cz
Rates: 4,500–5,600kc

A small boutique hotel situated on the Royal Way, 'The Golden Well' only has two double rooms and four suites. This 16th-century building has an incredibly ornate façade with statues, emblems and Baroque swirls. Internally, the rooms are furnished with simple, heavy wooden furniture and dark wooden floors, while many of the original features are retained, including painted wooden ceilings and vaults. Its location is very central but it is on the tourist track, so it can be quite noisy at times. Particularly irritating are the loud exclamations of delight at the tacky souvenirs being hawked all around. The basement restaurant is open to the public and serves Czech and international cuisine in its Romanesque cellar, but it is really only worth popping in for a quick drink. Reasonably priced for where it is and great fun if you want to be in the centre of everything.

> **Style 7, Atmosphere 7/8, Location 9**

U Zlatého Kola, Nerudova 28, P1.

Tel: 257 535 490 www.thegoldenwheel.com
Rates: 5,120–8,320kc

'The Golden Wheel' is a small foothill to Prague Castle's Everest.

Found on Nerudova Street, part of the Royal Way, at the base of the castle walls, this late 2003 newcomer provides substance and style – like its neighbour the Neruda. What the hotel has done is manage to bring a touch of class to this tourist thoroughfare. With only 17 rooms, U Zlatéhola Kola hasn't crammed in the numbers, but instead this sensitively restored townhouse exudes space and privacy. The rooms on the upper floors look up towards the castle walls and St Vitus's Cathedral, or across to the Petrin tower and its surrounding park. Again, in striking similarity to its neighbour, it has a stylish little café which sells ridiculously rich hot chocolates and proper Italian coffee. What the hotel achieves is a successful amalgamation of modern and traditional styles, where designer modern furnishings work with traditional painted ceilings.

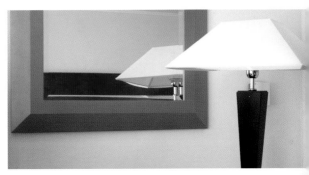

Style 8/9, Atmosphere 8, Location 8

eat...

The quality of food in Prague has always been a contentious issue. Some find it truly awful, whereas others extol the rich, natural pantry the country has to offer. The truth is that traditional Czech food is unlikely to be at the top of any gourmet's list – frequently over-cooked and lacking in any real flavour – but, on the plus side, it will fill you up. Traditional Czech dishes include wild boar, duck, carp or perch, red cabbage and dumplings. Sauces rich in cream and butter and over-generous portions could play havoc with your health if you're exposed long enough!

Since the lifting of the Iron Curtain the food has improved. Modern Czech cooking uses the same rich meats but combines them with more delicate sauces and ensures that they are prepared in a way that enhances the flavours. However, finding the better restaurants can still be a struggle. If you want to enjoy a traditional meal, there are three options.

The first is the beer hall, where you will sit at long tables next to total strangers, eating traditional stews and lumps of unidentifiable meat in the knowledge that the food serves purely as a countermeasure to alcoholic oblivion. None has been listed in this section, but U Medvídků and Radegast (see Drink) are both good examples.

The second option is to eat at one of the 'authentic' themed restaurants in the centre, which are often geared towards tourists and cater to the needs of large tour groups. The food will sound delicious – sauces laden with berries and *foïe gras* – but on arrival sometimes tends to be a little tasteless and rather too heavy. U Maltézských Rytířů and U Modré Kachničky are two of the top tourist-orientated restaurants and offer a genuine experience.

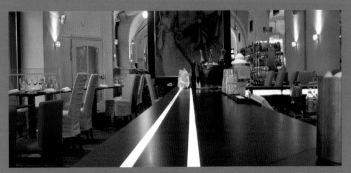

But there is a third, much more appetizing way to eat here if you know where to look. There is no need to eat badly in Prague any more – the city now caters to the most sophisticated and demanding of tastes. Since the Velvet Revolution, international cooking has arrived in the country, with restaurants ranging from Italian to Afghan. These newcomers will still provide the visitor to Prague with a new experience, since they show the influence of indigenous Czech cuisine in their choice of ingredients and styles of cooking. The French restaurants in particular display a heavy bias towards traditional Czech ingredients, making the most of the rich and plentiful game on offer. Unfortunately, however, although the Czech restaurants now produce dishes of a high standard, they still lag behind the more international restaurants in terms of sheer quality.

The ratings given in this section are a result of our first-hand experience of all the restaurants recommended here. Points for food were awarded for quality, choice and presentation. With regard to service, efficiency, speed and courteousness were paramount. We judged a restaurant's atmosphere according to its style, friendliness of the staff, how busy it was and the general ambience of the evening. The price given for each restaurant is based on the cost of an average two-course meal for one, with half a bottle of wine, including service and local taxes.

Our top 10 restaurants in Prague are:
1. Kampa Park
2. Le Bistrot de Marlène
3. Allegro
4. Flambée
5. Alcron
6. La Perle de Prague
7. Hergetova Cihelná
8. Rybi Trh
9. Opera Grill
10. V Zátiší

Our top five for food are:
1. Allegro
2. Kampa Park
3. Le Bistrot de Marlène
4. Alcron
5. V Zátiší

Our top five for service are:
1. Allegro
2. Flambée
3. Opera Grill
4. Le Bistrot de Marlène
5. La Perle de Prague

Our top five for atmosphere are:
1. Hergetova Cihelná
2. Kampa Park
3. Le Bistrot de Marlène
4. Divini's
5. Le Saint Jacques

A very comfortable fish restaurant with only seven tables and 22 covers, so with such limited space you'll need to book ahead. Based on an art deco concept, which extends throughout the hotel, a colourful mural of turn-of-the-century Prague life covers one wall. The room is dotted with interesting lamps and ornaments that create an intimate atmosphere with the aid of softened lighting. In 2002 it was rated as the best restaurant in Prague by *Gourmet*, the Czech equivalent to Zagat's restaurant guide. At first glance the menu is interesting, but on closer inspection it is superb. The dishes are constructed in innovative and appealing ways, delivering a consummate array of taste sensations and textures, with many incorporating *foïe gras* or black truffles in interesting combinations. The wine list is detailed, with a comprehensive selection of New and Old World wines, complete with thorough descriptions and recommendations. A five-course gourmet menu is on offer with selected wine, provided by the glass to complement each dish. In short, the food is outstanding, especially if you are a fan of fish. Everything is cooked to perfection, the plates are immaculate, the service attentive and friendly… but carnivores beware: this menu is entirely dedicated to fish and seafood. Meat is not an option. If that's okay with you, it seems to have everything going for it, except that it

is just off the lobby of the Radisson SAS hotel. Dinner can be interrupted by the hustle and bustle of a working hotel: loud businessmen meeting in the lobby next door sometimes break up the slightly sterile atmosphere. But, if you can stomach eating in a chain hotel, then it is a truly delightful gastronomic experience.

Food 9/10, Service 9, Atmosphere 7/8

Allegro, Four Seasons Hotel, Veleslavínova 2, P1.
Tel: 221 427 000 www.fourseasons.com/prague/dining
Open: 11.30am–midnight daily   2,000kc

Fine dining at its best – the Four Seasons has created a restaurant that has had most critics raving. The Allegro's culinary expertise is beyond question, the Mediterranean/Czech fusion created by chef Vito Mollica is superb. The rich flavours and array of taste sensations are truly extraordinary and the dishes are prepared to perfection. As one would expect from a Four Seasons hotel, the service is immaculate and watchful – the diner will rarely go without but the attention level is still discreet. The one downside to the Allegro is the fact that it does sit in a major international hotel; while the restaurant is well designed, it just can't shake off that slight air of sterility. But come the summer when guests can take dinner on the small terrace overlooking the river and the castle, all reservations can be dismissed.

Rumour has it that it might just achieve a coveted Michelin star in the near future. At its best on a balmy summer's evening for dinner on the terrace.

Food 9/10, Service 9/10, Atmosphere 8

Arzenal, Valentinská 11, P1.
Tel: 224 814 099
Open: 10am–midnight daily   850kc

A smart Thai restaurant and design shop just around the corner from the Rudolfinium. The menu is typically Thai, and aficionados will recognize many classics, including *tom yum* soup, *phad Thai* and green curry. Arzenal is one of the few places in Prague where you can come to experience a genuine chilli hit; however, its real selling-point is the extraordinary glassware, cutlery and trimmings on your table made by young Czech designers. If you fall in love with these sometimes extraordinary pieces you can buy one; they can be purchased from the shop. This won't be the best Thai restaurant you will ever visit, but it does provide a refreshing and light alternative to the much of the city's more traditional, heavy cuisines.

Food 7, Service 7, Atmosphere 7/8

Barock, Pařížská 24, P1.
Tel: 222 329 221
Open: 8.30am–1am Monday–Friday;
10am–1am Saturday–Sunday   1,500kc

One of two ultra-glamorous and sophisticated restaurants found on this fashionable shopping street. In summer, you can enjoy sitting outside and watching Prague's wealthy shoppers glide by in the sunshine. After dark, and in winter, the vibrant mix of clientele from the higher echelons of Czech and ex-pat society gather inside to discuss the day's events over dinner. The interior is framed with black and white fashion prints, large gilt mirrors and ornate crystal chandeliers. The décor juxtaposes the antique and the contemporary, melding into a French-style brasserie. The menu is Asian in concept with an emphasis on sushi, but with a fine selection of Thai and Japanese dishes. The wine list draws from cellars around the world, but we recommend acquainting yourself with the excellent *sake*. The food is delicious, innovative and beautiful to look at; and the service is prompt and friendly.

Food 8, Service 8, Atmosphere 8

Bazaar, Nerudova 40, P1.
Tel: 257 535 050 www.restaurantbazaar.cz
Open: 6pm–midnight daily   900kc

A loud and lively vaulted brick restaurant, Bazaar is close to the castle, at the top end of Nerudova Street (this involves a stiff walk uphill). Recently acquired by the group that brought you Kampa Park, Cihelna and Square, it promises to become more of a destination. Its roof-terrace bar makes a great place to kick off a summer's evening before descending to the intimate restaurant. During the week it is reasonably quiet but at the weekend it jolts into life, attracting diners from far-flung corners of the globe as well as smart locals and ex-pats drawn from the surrounding embassy district. The restaurant has an international bias with an Italian emphasis, but also draws on other European and North African cuisines. The food is nothing exceptional, but the service is attentive and the atmosphere buzzing. Definitely worth a visit on a summer's evening, since this is when the beautiful people come out to play, sipping cocktails as the sun drifts down, with Charles Bridge bathed in glorious light.

Food 6/7, Service 7, Atmosphere 8

Bellevue, Smetanovo nábřeži 18, P1.
Tel: 222 221 443
Open: noon–3pm, 5.30–11pm Monday–Saturday;
11am–3.30pm, 7–11pm Sunday   1,500kc

A superb location for this aptly named restaurant overlooking Charles Bridge and the Vltava River, and with a clear view up to the castle; and Bellevue also boasts a sun-splashed terrace for those warm lunches and balmy summer evenings. It comes from the same stable as V Zátiší, Circle Line and Mlynec, which means that while the food is delicious the atmosphere is sometimes

stiff and formal. The restaurant is set up in the grand tradition, with extremely attentive if somewhat aloof service, elegant and tasteful décor, and its appeal belongs to an older and more reserved generation. Ornately furnished, it has huge windows looking out over the river, which create a light room with delightful views. The food is international, drawing on ingredients from around the world, from New Zealand lamb to Maine lobster. The menu is eclectic, and displays advanced gastronomic intentions, whil it also adheres to the basic principles of traditional Czech cuisine. Couples might enjoy a civilized Sunday champagne jazz brunch, but don't expect it to help the hangover.

Food 8/9, Service 8, Atmosphere 6

Le Bistrot de Marlène, Plavecká 4, P2.
Tel: 224 921 853 www.bistrotdemarlene.cz
Open: noon–2.30pm, 7–10.30pm.
Closed Saturday lunch, Sunday.   1,200kc

Situated 20 minutes' walk from the centre, this is arguably

Prague's finest restaurant, and a regular haunt of the sophisticated ex-pat community. Many deals have been won or lost here, as high-powered businessmen and politicians engage in charged arguments while being served superb French cuisine. The restaurant itself oozes sleek, elegant refinement, with intimate lighting, fabric draped from the ceiling and a cosy layout. The menu is based on French country cuisine, but adopts a fresh approach, placing emphasis on the quality of the ingredients and exquisite preparation. The wine list has been created to suit the different dishes; the emphasis is definitely French, but there are some good-quality European, Chilean and Czech wines to pander to more international tastes. Recommended for its excellent food, attentive service – and as probably the finest dining experience in the city.

Food 9, Service 9, Atmosphere 9

Brasserie Ullmann, Letenské Sady 341, P7.
Tel: 233 378 200 www.letenskyzamecek.cz
Open: 11am–11pm daily   450kc

A small designer brasserie set in Letenské Sady, a park stretching down from the castle to the river on the north side of the city. Forming part of a refurbished chateau, it is exactly the sort of restaurant you just stumble across. Upstairs is an exceptionally smart, reservations-only restaurant, while in the garden there is a simpler terrace restaurant where you can enjoy beer in plastic cups amonge topless teenagers. All were refurbished in 2001. Inside, Brasserie Ullmann is simple and modern, retaining some of the Art Deco characteristics that the city exudes. A fair amount of glass means that the lines are fresh and uncomplicated. The menu is seasonal and the specials change at different points in the year to incorporate truffles, oysters and seasonal game. During our visit the menu included an interesting combination of Czech and French dishes, making good use of local goose and rabbit. The staff are proactive and friendly, serving some tasty food and a wonderfully rich onion soup. It's a great place to come for a head-clearing Saturday morning walk, with spectacular views of the Old Town stretched out below to be followed by a decent lunch.

Food 7/8, Service 8, Atmosphere 7/8

Le Café Colonial, Široká 6, P1.
Tel: 224 818 322
Open: 10am–midnight daily   900kc

A colourful restaurant deep in the heart of the Jewish Quarter, whose walls are painted in deep reds, blues, yellows and greens. Huge wrought-iron, Art Deco chandeliers hang from the ceiling, while the diners underneath are seated at classically designed tables with matching chairs. The stylish menu bodes well and heralds a high standard of cuisine that displays immense attention to detail. Le Café Colonial offers a tempting selection of dishes drawn from a predominantly French menu, but tinged with international and regional flourishes. The wine list is complete, with a small selection of Czech and some reasonably priced Italian and French wines. What is so refreshing about the restaurant is that it offers good food in an informal atmosphere, especially as the restaurant spills over into a café area – ideal for a long, leisurely lunch.

Food 8, Service 7/8, Atmosphere 8

Café La Veranda, Elišky Krásnohorské 2, P1.
Tel: 224 814 733 www.laveranda.cz
Open: 11am–11pm Monday–Saturday; 4–11pm Sunday   900kc

One of the new generation of smart café/restaurants that are springing up all over Prague. Located in trendy Josefov, Café La Veranda is the epitome of a contemporary restaurant in a fashionable area. The basic layout relies on a contrast of colours, combined with architecturally clean lines. Large windows looking up towards the street throw light into the room and give this subterranean restaurant an airy, illuminated feeling. The menu is based on an East-meets-West fusion, and is free of all fats and fatty meats. Café La Veranda prides itself on its bold cooking and the innovative combinations of dishes, using the freshest ingredients it can lay its hands on. A selection of different menus (including a *dégustation* menu) is designed to reflect award-winning chef Radek David's interest in different taste combinations and sensations.

Food 8, Service 8, Atmosphere 8

Café Savoy, Vitězná 5, P5.
Tel: 257 329 860 www.cafesavoy.cz
Open: 8am–midnight daily   1,000kc

A charming and elegant café/restaurant, located across the river from the National Theatre and now splendidly restored as one of Prague's most fashionable eateries. In the summer they lay out a few tables on the terrace at the front, overlooking the busy square, making it a great place to have lunch. Inside there is an

ultra-contemporary interior with designer furniture, modern wall-lighting schemes and swathes of red fabric hanging from the ceiling. The food is delicious, with a choice of indulgent dishes borrowed from different cuisines; these include oysters, lobster and high-quality fish. The service is charmingly professional; we were accorded just the right amount of attention. As the restaurant lies slightly outside the normal tourist area, you are more likely to be surrounded by elegant Czechs and businessmen than guidebook clutchers. A great to watch the locals go by.

Food 8/9, Service 8, Atmosphere 8

Circle Line, Malostranské náměsti 12, P1.
Tel: 257 530 021
Open: noon–3pm, 5.30–11pm daily   1,500kc

The second of the restaurants in the V Zátiší chain, Circle Line stands in the corner of this prestigious square beneath the castle. The main dining room, set under a pink vaulted ceiling, is uncluttered and elegant in its simplicity, although the tiled floor and raised ceilings can lead to some rather noisy acoustics. As with its sister establishments (Bellevue, Mlynec and V Zátiší) the emphasis is very much on the grand dining experience, which may mean a rather formal meal. The menu is dedicated to the gourmet palate: international in style with a definite bias towards French cuisine, its rich sauces and elaborate ingredients. There

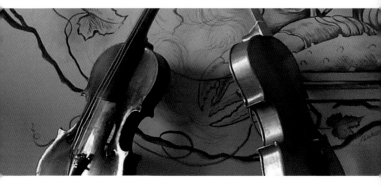

are classic dishes, *foïe gras* as well as more imaginative offerings such as rabbit *carpaccio*. The most suitable wine for each dish is suggested, while a separate gourmet menu gives a glass of different wine to complement each of the seven courses. The food is delectable, exquisitely prepared, presented and cooked to perfection. And, as with its siblings, the service is efficient and attentive but sometimes rather cold and formal.

Food 9, Service 8/9, Atmosphere 7

David, Tržiště 21, P1.
Tel: 257 533 109 www.restaurant-david.cz
Open: 11.30am–11pm daily   900kc

Nestled away in the backstreets beneath the Castle, this is a gourmet's paradise. The delicately prepared dishes are beautifully served by charming and friendly staff. There is a small terrace outside for warm evenings and inside an intimate restaurant for those seeking a gastronomic experience, packed with antique furniture and original paintings. The French/Czech menu is not extensive; instead it is very particular, crammed with freshly prepared, intricate dishes and subtle food combinations. The small restaurant is independently run: the *maître d'* and the chef who own it are on hand to ensure that everything is at its best and that you get the most out of your experience.

Food 8, Service 9, Atmosphere 7/8

Divini's, Tynska 23, P1.
Tel: 224 808 318 www.divinis.cz
Open: 11am–4pm, 6pm–midnight   1,200kc

Originally a wine shop, this little restaurant is rapidly drawing in
the great and the good for its excellent Italian food and fine
selection of wines. A short but regularly changing menu offers
original and interesting but simple dishes. The simplicity is rather
a necessity as the small kitchen doesn't allow for over elabora-
tion in order to serve the 10 or so tables. The owner, Pino
Confessa, is often in evidence, offering advice on the excellent
wines and discussing Italian sartorial elegance, engaging the clientele in long, animated conversations. The staff are typically Italian
and love a good chat – so the food sometimes takes a long time
to arrive. However, what it certainly means is a buzzing atmosphere. It hasn't been here for very long but it is bound to
become an institution.

Food 8/9, Service 8, Atmosphere 8/9

Don Giovanni, Karolíny Světlé 34, P1.
Tel: 222 222 060 www.dongiovanni.cz
Open 11am–midnight daily   1,000kc

It is almost impossible to escape the name 'Don Giovanni' in
Prague, ever since the première of Mozart's opera was held in

the Estates Theatre. The Czechs try to cash in at every opportunity, a particular favourite of ours being the 'Don Giovanni puppet opera'. However, this is a good Italian restaurant close to Charles Bridge, its unassuming exterior giving the impression of a tourist trap instead of the decent restaurant it actually is. In fact, inside it provides a rather formal dining experience; dark wooden floors and ornate Italianate tables and chairs give an air of sophistication and bygone elegance. The walls are covered with portraits of some of the more glamorous and renowned Czechs, and are constantly added to as someone new hits the heights. The menu is quintessentially Italian with a fine selection of pasta, fish and seafood, while the wine list boasts a cross-section of the country's cellars. The food is not of the highest quality but is well prepared and comforting – one of the better Italians in town, if perhaps not the liveliest.

Food 7/8, Service 7/8, Atmosphere 7

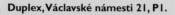

Duplex, Václavské námesti 21, P1.
Tel: 224 232 319 www.duplexduplex.cz
Open: 11am–11pm daily   900kc

A light, airy rooftop restaurant with an expansive terrace that affords spectacular views over Wenceslas Square and the western part of the city. The interior is filled with flowing white drapes, modish furniture and wooden floors, while large windows take advantage of the views. Duplex is chic and stylish, populated by well-dressed Czech and international 30-some-things. A Pacific-Asian fusion menu takes inspiration from China,

Thailand, Hawaii and Polynesia, combining international concepts with traditional Czech ingredients. The result is interesting but doesn't quite hit the heights. Alongside the restaurant is a sophisticated bar, and once the meal has settled you can go upstairs to the fashionable nightclub. At times it can be quiet, but at the weekend the club really kicks into action. The street entrance is rather anonymous, but once you've taken the elevator to the sixth floor you'd be forgiven for feeling slightly daunted.

Food 7/8, Service 7/8, Atmosphere 8

Flambée, Husova 5, P1.
Tel: 224 248 512 www.flambee.cz
Open: 11.30am–1am daily   2,000kc

Definitely one of Prague's more elegant and accomplished restaurants. The cellar was converted in 1993, winning international awards for its design, and was refurbished after the 2002 floods. The ambience is reasonably formal, which means that the clientele tends to be slightly older and grander than elsewhere, but is one of the more gourmet venues in town and does make a great romantic destination. The food is superb, beautifully prepared and arrives looking like a work of art. The menu is designed to appeal to those in the know, with the option of a special five course set menu specially selected by the chef, and there are more truffle and *foïe gras* combinations than you can shake a stick at. There is an extensive wine list with an inordinate amount of top French wines. The service is first rate and boasts one of the few sommeliers in the city, on hand to furnish you with the best wines to enhance your meal. The bad news is that you definitely pay for the privilege of eating here; the good news is that it's worth it!

Food 9, Service 9, Atmosphere 8/9

Francouzská, Obecní Dům, nám Republiky 5, P1.
Tel: 222 002 770 www.obecnidum.cz
Open: noon–4pm, 6pm–11pm daily   1,450kc

Perhaps the most elegant restaurant in Prague, set within the Municipal House – one of the city's most impressive Art Nouveau buildings. The dining room is a beautiful large, open room with stunning chandeliers and wall lights, all beneath a delightful painted 30-foot ceiling. Settle into the dark green leather banquettes overlooking expanses of pristine white tablecloths covered in fine bohemian crystal, and drift back a century in time. The menu is a mix of traditional Czech and world cuisine; specialities include *foïe gras*, lobster bisque and *coq au vin*. The service is formal, everything is done properly and the highest standard is insisted on. It can seem slightly over-the-top, but completes the turn-of-the-century feel. In the same building are equally smart café and Pilsen restaurants as well as a beautiful concert hall. The restaurant runs packages including tickets to a concert and a set three-course menu for 1,600kc – good value for a night of sophisticated food and classical entertainment.

Food 8, Service 8/9, Atmosphere 8

Hergetova Cihelná, Cihelná 2b, P1.
Tel: 257 535 534 www.cihelna.com
Open: 9am–2am daily   900kc

A younger sibling of the legendary Kampa Park, Cihelná has impressed in its own right. Devastated a week before its scheduled opening by the floods of 2002, it has re-emerged with a vengeance. While it shares Kampa Park's stunning views of Charles Bridge and the Old Town, its menu and concept differ. Cihelná has been set up as a bar/lounge and restaurant, shifting the emphasis away from dining to socializing – but that's not to say that there is any shirking on the quality, presentation and flavour of the food. The restaurant is spread over two floors: upstairs is going to be restructured as a separate pizzeria while downstairs is the long bar, main dining room and terrace. The terrace in particular is a delight in the summer, where you can enjoy a wonderful summer lunch or balmy evening. As one has come to expect from this restaurant group, style is of paramount importance. Like Kampa Park, Cihelná is full of Prague's movers

and shakers, as well as some of the city's better-informed and
well-heeled visitors. The menu is an eclectic combination of
tastes, merging the flavours of the Far East with those of Italy
and Central Europe.

Food 8/9, Service 8/9, Atmosphere 9

Kampa Park, Na Kampá 8b, P1.
Tel: 257 532 685/6 www.kampapark.com
Open: 11.30am–1am daily   1,400kc

The *grande dame* of Prague's gourmet scene, Kampa Park opened
in the early 1990s, and has consistently ranked among the city's
restaurant elite ever since. Founded by Nils Jebens, it has
become the flagship of a culinary empire that includes Square
and Cihelná, as well as recent acquisitions La Provence and

Bazaar. Fêted for its high standards, Kampa's menu is a real treat – not only does it draw from the Czech Republic's natural pantry, but it has also has created an almost seamless amalgamation of cuisines from around the world. As has become typical in New Europe, the highest levels of cuisine borrow ingredients and ideas from the Far East. Like the food, the design of the restaurant is modern and stylish. Split into three sections, the main restaurant is restrained and sophisticated, the smaller dining room overlooking the river is quiet and elegant while the water-level terrace is light, airy and relaxing. Kampa Park is a Prague institution that retains its popularity year-in, year-out; definitely worth a visit, but book ahead.

Food 9, Service 8/9, Atmosphere 9

Kogo, Na Příkopě 22, P1.
Tel: 221 451 259
Open: 11am–11pm daily   800kc

The second restaurant in the ever-expanding Kogo chain has proved to be one of the most successful in Prague, set in the courtyard of a new shopping centre off the busy shopping thoroughfare of Na Příkopě. Outside is a huge seating area, while the interior is smart and crisp. The restaurant is the haunt of top politicians, media execs and successful ex-pats; the byword here is definitely glamour. A constantly buzzing atmosphere means that this is the place to see and be seen. The service is incredibly

quick and efficient, yet the waiters are still able to add that friendly, personal touch. The great thing about Kogo is that the food is of a consistently high standard at realistic prices, and the selection of quintessential Italian dishes means that it is always in vogue. Kogo is ideal for either a long, protracted meal involving plenty of food and wine, or just a quick bite to eat pre- or post-theatre.

Food 8, Service 8, Atmosphere 9

U Malířů, Maltézské náměstí 11, P1.
Tel: 257 530 000 www.umaliru.cz
Open: 11.30am–midnight daily   2,000kc

An intimate, romantic French restaurant hiding away in a quaint, cobbled square. The house was built in the 15th century and first opened as a restaurant in 1543, making it one of the oldest restaurants in Prague. The dozen or so tables sit under a beautifully frescoed, vaulted ceiling. The low lighting and classical music waft nonchalantly over sophisticated diners reclining in deep red chairs and banquettes. Small leaded windows and frescoed walls all help to lend the place an air of intimacy and old-world elegance. The limited menu combines a choice of four starters and four fish and meat courses, as well as a selection of three set menus, so if you're picky then you may have a few problems. The opulent food is good but not extraordinary; however, the actual execution of the meal is highly professional: you are treated to

amuse bouches – sorbets between courses – which help to create the impression of a special dining experience. But of course, you pay for the privilege – U Malířů is renowned for being one of the most expensive restaurants in the city.

Food 8, Service 9, Atmosphere 8

U Maltézských Rytířů, Prokopská 10, P1.
Tel: 257 530 075
Open 11am–11pm daily   900kc

A traditional Czech restaurant in a quiet street leading to Maltézské náměstí, which is a beautiful little square adjacent to Charles Bridge. Upstairs is a small bar area with a couple of tables, but make sure you get a table in the basement or your

journey will be wasted. The cellar is split into two small, candlelit rooms hung with old portraits and fitted with antique furniture, creating an incredibly intimate environment. There is a sort of medieval glamour attached to the place; however, it is mentioned in every guidebook to Prague so consequently it is always packed with tourists. This is one of the few traditional Czech restaurants with a romantic ambience and decent food (although, as is so often the case in the Czech Republic, it can be overcooked). The manageress is exceptionally welcoming and friendly, and will bend over backwards to accommodate her guests; however, service can be slightly lackadaisical on a busy evening. U Maltézských Rytířů is a lovely romantic restaurant, but overrun with tourists.

Food 7, Service 7/8, Atmosphere 8

Mlynec, Novotného lávka 9, P1.
Tel: 221 082 208 www.pfd.cz
Open: noon–3pm, 5.30–11pm daily   1,300kc

Having been washed away in the floods of 2002, Mlynec has been painstakingly reconstructed to resemble an early 1990s hotel restaurant. Green carpets patterned with gold *fleur de lys*, antiqued curtains and tapestries are juxtaposed with a heavily spotlighted ceiling. That said, Mlynec is far from ordinary or

depressing. The food, in its wonderful combinations of traditional Czech and refreshing Far Eastern dishes, is superb. Presentation, as with all the restaurants in this group (Bellevue, Circle Line and V Zátiší), is immaculate; it all looks far too good to eat. Wedged between two of Prague's clubs most popular with foreign visitors, and a few steps from Charles Bridge, it inevitably attracts wealthy tourists at weekends and business diners during the week. Everyone comes to take full advantage of the splendid views of the river, the bridge and the castle.

Food 8/9, Service 9, Atmosphere 7

U Modré Kachničky 2, Michalská 16, P1.
Tel: 224 213 418 www.modrekachnicky.cz
Open: 11.30am–11.30pm daily   700kc

The second version of this Prague dining institution is set centrally in the Old Town, not far from Old Town Square. U Modré Kachničky is definitely one of Prague's better Czech restaurants, specializing in game and duck in particular, hence the name ('The Blue Duck'). Occupying two floors, and playing 1930s and '40s

swing and jazz music, it is a romantic little place. Downstairs is darker and more intimate, while upstairs can be used to cater for larger parties and groups. The menu is quintessentially Czech, with a predictable emphasis on duck, but other options include steak, game and fish. The wine list has all the traditional bottles found in either a Czech or French cellar, and luckily the waiters are knowledgeable, and can help you choose the best wine to complement your meal. The food is very good – surprisingly so for Czech food – if somewhat heavy. This restaurant is one of our favourites, and remember it wouldn't be a true local meal if you didn't leave feeling several stone heavier.

Food 7/8, Service 8, Atmosphere 8

Opera Grill, Karolíny Světlé 35, P1.
Tel: 222 220 518 www.operagrill.cz
Open: 6pm–2am daily   1,600kc

A small but renowned restaurant on this trendy little street, seating just over 20 people, so intimacy is assured. The sumptuous dining room is filled with faded, old-world elegance: chandeliers hang from the ceiling, candles glow on tables while the windows to the outside world are shuttered, transporting you back in time. It's not immediately obvious how you get in (you ring a bell to one side of a gated corridor), and this adds to the exclusivity that the place oozes. Undoubtedly one of the most romantic restaurants in Prague, the old-fashioned armchairs and banquettes, gilt mirrors and pianist tinkling away in the corner all help to create a seductively personal atmosphere. The *maître d'* and owner is charming, attentive and talkative; he expects everyone to have a memorable evening and a complete experience. Incorporating a mix of cuisines, the menu manages to combine a delicious blend of tastes, but with a Czech–French emphasis. The wine selection is drawn from the finest Czech vineyards, with some more renowned European wines for the less brave. While the food is very good, the enveloping atmosphere and personal service are the real selling points.

Food 7/8, Service 9, Atmosphere 9

Palffy Palac, Valdštejnská 14, P1.
Tel: 257 530 522
Open: 11am–midnight daily   1,000kc

Slightly off the main tourist route, to one side of Malostranské

náměsti, this classic restaurant is situated in an old palace. To reach it, you have to climb past the music schools, up a large baroque staircase (bathed in candlelight at night), to the top floor. The main dining room has a beautiful gilded chandelier hanging from its high ceiling. Every table is slightly different; some have their own fruit bowls, others fresh flowers. The tables and chairs again differ from table to table, very subtly, generating the feeling that each dining experience is unique and special. The walls are covered in portraits and photographs of Prague in its halcyon days, and some of its past worthies. The international menu is based around traditional Czech ideals; we enjoyed a delicate wild duck *carpaccio* and roast quail. In the summer months the large terrace is opened up so diners can enjoy views over the rooftops towards the Old Town below; what better place to start an evening, while you sip a cool glass of Moravian wine? Palffy Palac is a great place for a romantic dinner, with fun and friendly service.

Food 8, Service 8, Atmosphere 8/9

Parnas, Smetanovo nábřeži 2, P1.
Tel: 224 218 493
Open: 6pm–midnight daily   900kc

A magnificent Art Deco room with wonderful ornate wood panelled walls, stone floor and flattering ceiling and wall lights. Large windows overlook the river and up towards the castle, illuminated against the sky line. This is the sister restaurant to the famous Café Slavia next door. Smart, dark wooden Art Deco furniture is beautifully offset by the crisp, white linen tablecloths; it's as if you have stepped back in time to the beginning of the 20th century. The Czech menu concentrates on meat and game, since these inevitably appeal to the tourists, and the rabbit and goulash are difficult to beat for taste. The Czech wine list complements the food, but some more established tipples are on offer for those a little unsure of the local viniculture. A pianist in the corner helps personalize the atmosphere. It is worth a trip for the experience of dining in this wonderful setting, and you certainly won't be disappointed by the food. Just a stone's throw from the National Theatre, it's a great place for a post-opera dinner.

Food 8, Service 8, Atmosphere 8/9

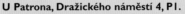

U Patrona, Dražického náměstí 4, P1.
Tel: 257 530 725
Open: 11am–midnight daily   1,000kc

A small restaurant set in a townhouse just to the north of Charles Bridge, U Patrona was totally devastated by the floods of 2002. It reopened a year later having undergone a total facelift. Downstairs is a light and spacious dining room, simply and elegantly furnished, while upstairs seems a little more sophisticated with a tiny, intimate balcony for two. One of the pleasures of eating here is being able to see the chefs at work in the kitchen while being waited on hand and foot. U Patrona is old-fashioned dining in Prague at its most intimate and exclusive – unfortunately, because of its location, there are lots of American and Japanese tourists who would agree. The French menu highlights the easy fusion between traditional Gallic cooking and the Czech Republic's natural larder, as the kitchen makes full use of and perfectly prepares the best of the indigenous game.

Food 8, Service 8/9, Atmosphere 8

● **La Perle de Prague, Rašínovo nábřeži 80, P2.**
Tel: 221 984 160 www.laperle.cz
Open: noon–2pm, 7–10.30pm. Closed Sunday and
Monday lunch.   1,300kc

Set at the top of Frank Gehry's Dancing House, Prague's most talked about example of modern architecture, the restaurant has fabulous views over the river and up towards the castle. The entrance is not immediately apparent, hidden inside a small, often quiet café to one side; but from here you are shown up to the seventh floor. La Perle is split over two floors; upstairs offers access to the terrace with a few tables for a pre- or post-dinner drink, or romantic rooftop liaisons. Downstairs a formal, elegant and modern interior sets the tone for the restaurant. The clientele is all well-to-do and smartly dressed – a good mix of well-heeled locals, international businessmen and the odd romantically inclined holiday-maker. The menu is primarily French, offering a broad selection of game, meat, fish and seafood, washed down with an extensive selection of French wine. The interior is fresh and crisp; everything is sleek and modern, with meticulous attention to detail.

Food 8/9, Service 9, Atmosphere 8/9

Pravda, Pařížská 17, P1.
Tel: 222 326 303
Open: 8.30am–1am (2am Thursday–Friday) Monday–Friday;
10am–2am Saturday; 10am–1am Sunday   1,200kc

An incredibly glamorous restaurant on the fashionable shopping street Pařížská, opposite its sister restaurant Barock. It's designed and decorated in the style of a glamorous French brasserie, with pristine white tablecloths, a long, elegant bar and mirrors that increase the feeling of space. The food is international, mixing European and Asian cuisine to create interesting fusions of taste and texture. The evening brings a greater choice and a more intimate atmosphere, as lunch tends to be interrupted by passing tour groups. On a warm day, *al fresco* dining provides interesting people-watching opportunities. Although not as glamorous as its sister restaurant, it certainly attracts a well-heeled international and local crowd. The good wine list and cocktail menu ensure that you'll enjoy yourself late into the night.

Food 8, Service 8, Atmosphere 8

La Provence, Štupartská 9, P1.
Tel: 257 535 050 www.laprovence.cz
Open: 11am–1am daily   900kc

A sparingly lit basement restaurant with all the trappings of a rustic French bistro, La Provence has been amalgamated into the ever-expanding Kampa Park chain. Internally it has not been altered significantly, except for the removal of some clutter. The restaurant has always been known for its popularity and humming atmosphere, which results in part from the occasional live piano music and the cosy, intimate surroundings. The menu is essentially French with a smattering of classic international dishes, but whatever your preference there is an extensive choice.

The food is reasonably priced for reasonable quality, and you can have a good early evening dinner before delving into the entertainment of the 'triangle of sin'.

Food 6/7, Service 6/7, Atmosphere 7

Rasoi, Dlouhá 13, P1.
Tel: 222 328 400 www.rasoi.cz
Open: 11.30am–11.30pm daily   600kc

One of the few Indian establishments in the city centre, Rasoi's basement restaurant is surprisingly light and airy – the languid spread of the tables adds to the feeling of spaciousness. Murals of rural India and relaxing Indian music help to create an authentic feeling. At first glance the menu is not particularly inspiring – the dishes don't sound very exotic or potent. However, the food is unexpectedly good and fiery to match, providing a change from the milder Czech food. Another advantage of eating here is the proximity of Bombay Cocktail Bar above it, which is under the same ownership and provides a great venue for a pre- or post-dinner drink. Service can be slightly lackadaisical – you never want to see waiters kicking the kitchen doors open. Nevertheless, Rasoi is good for a change, and essential for those who just can't leave their curry addiction behind them.

Food 7, Service 6, Atmosphere 6

Rybí Trh, Týn 5, P1.

Tel: 224 895 447 www.flambee.cz
Open: 11am–midnight daily   1,100kc

Tucked away behind Old Town Square in a quiet courtyard full of little bars and restaurants, Rybi Trh is famous for its delicious fish. In the summer the restaurant has a charming outdoor terrace – a perfect suntrap for balmy lunches alongside *fashionistas* hiding behind designer sunglasses. The choice consists of seafood and fish, bar a couple of meat dishes for the rabid carnivores and, for Prague, a good selection of vegetable side dishes. The extensive range of dishes is exquisitely prepared and delicious. A wide-ranging wine list includes an interesting selection of Old and New World wines, all taken from Rybí Trh's wine shop next door and all available to buy. It is well worth a quick trip if you are interested in stocking up on some fine Moravian wines before you return home. Inside the décor is relatively simple; fish tanks set off the impressive selection of fish laid out on crushed ice. The fine food is relatively expensive but good for a sunny summer lunch or a romantic evening meal.

Food 9, Service 8/9, Atmosphere 8

Le Saint Jacques, Jakubská 4, P1.

Tel: 222 322 685 www.saint-jacques.cz
Open: noon–3pm, 6pm–midnight.
Closed Saturday/Sunday lunch.   1,200kc

A small, backstreet French bistro, lodged between some of Prague's livelier student bars. Le St Jacques food is good but the real reason to visit is the pair of musicians, a pianist and violinist who are found in the restaurant every night talking, joking and taking requests from the diners. Even if the restaurant is quiet they'll liven it up with tunes ranging from Cole Porter to haunting gypsy ballads. Towards the end of the evening, once sufficient alcohol has flowed, they coax diners onto their feet to dance between the tables by flickering candlelight. The classically French menu is filled with customary dishes: frog's legs, snails and an excellent *coquilles Saint-Jacques* are available, all complemented by a selection of French regional wines. This is definitely one for the incurable romantics.

Food 7/8, Service 7/8, Atmosphere 9

Sarah Bernhardt, U Obecního domu 1, P1.
Tel: 222 195 195 www.sarah-bernhardt.cz
Open: noon–4pm, 6pm–midnight daily   1,250kc

A grandiose restaurant located in the fantastic Art Nouveau Hotel Paříž. The interior of the restaurant is partially clad in blue mosaic, which combines with original lighting fixtures, gilded stuccowork and dark wooden furniture to create a sophisticated and elegant setting. Sarah Bernhardt sets itself up as a grand dining experience: a pianist plays away while waiters scurry around diligently in a rather hushed manner, generating a rarefied atmos-

phere. The menu temptingly describes an accomplished mixture of French and Czech cuisine. On our visit a decidedly unappetizing-looking *amuse bouche* was presented, which somewhat worried us about what was to follow. But once this was polished off the remaining dishes were delectable melting pots of flavour. Sarah Bernhardt is recommended if your party includes the older generation, but is slightly too formal and reserved for a lively or romantic evening.

Food 8, Service 8/9, Atmosphere 7

Square, Malostranské náměstí 5, P1.
Tel: 257 532 109 www.squarerestaurant.cz
Open: 9am–1am (3am Thursday–Saturday) daily   800kc

Square, a modern restaurant/bar set in the heart of Mala Straná, opened in the summer of 2002, under the same ownership as Kampa Park, one of the most successful restaurants of the 1990s. The interior was designed by Bára Skorpilová, the same bright young architect who created Zaharada V Opeře, and in much the same style he has created a very fresh and contemporary space. There are various different areas to the restaurant: outside are two sections of terrace, one decked out with steel and chrome tables, the other with fibreglass armchairs and sofas; while inside are distinct dining and drinking areas. The food is based on Mediterranean cuisine, and has a first-class selection of *tapas*, as well as traditional favourites from the Czech Republic and France. The venue is incredibly chic, suited to many purposes: good for entertaining clients, it's equally appropriate for an intimate dinner for two, or a relaxed evening out with friends. A good selection of wines, cocktails and whiskies is on offer to help evenings run fluidly. Square is one of a new breed of sophisticated, contemporary restaurants in Prague that successfully combines fashion with food.

Food 8, Service 8/9, Atmosphere 8/9

Universal, V Jirchářích 6, P1.
Tel: 224 934 416
Open: 11am–1am daily
700kc

A bistro in the heart of SoNa, behind the National Theatre, Universal is an atmospheric little place with purposefully plain

wooden tables and chairs and a bizarre array of decoration on the walls. A long French poem winds around the room, while a moulded elephant's head hangs near the traffic lights. It just doesn't make a lot of sense! Happily, it does offer excellent French cuisine. The menu is not particularly inventive but we enjoyed an excellent lamb with goat's cheese and thyme, and a delectable salmon tartare. Owned and run by a very pleasant couple who are on hand to ensure that everything runs smoothly. It has a mixed clientele of locals, ex-pats and the occasional adventurous tourist who has escaped from the predictability of the town centre.

Food 7/8, Service 7, Atmosphere 7

V Zátiší, Liliová 1, P1.
Tel: 222 221 155 www.pfd.cz
Open: noon–3pm, 5.30–11pm daily   1,700kc

V Zátiší is the third restaurant in the series after Bellevue and Circle Line, and is regarded as one of the best, if not the best, restaurant in the entire country. The food is undeniably fabulous, superbly cooked and packed with flavour, but we felt slightly let down by the ambience. As with the other members of this chain, the emphasis is on the grand dining experience, exquisite food and formal service, catering to a decidedly up-market clientele. This may sound ideal, but we found the atmosphere slightly stilted, with conversations conducted in hushed tones. The menu offers an eclectic mix of international and domestic fare, drawing

ingredients from across the world to create an array of superb dishes. Two set menus are available with wine included to complement the dishes. Expensive by Prague standards but no more so than an average London restaurant.

Food 9, Service 9, Atmosphere 7

Zahrada v Opeře, Legerova 75, P1.
Tel: 224 239 685 www.zahradavopere.cz
Open: 11.30am–1am daily   1,100kc

Another of our favourites, and part of a great night out if combined with a trip to the State Opera (hence the name, 'Garden of the Opera') or as an individual experience. Recently dubbed 'the safest garden in the world', since the Americans went into Afghanistan this restaurant has been guarded by tanks and armed soldiers. Why? Well, it is directly beneath the Radio Free Europe headquarters, which specialize in broadcasting propaganda into Afghanistan and other Islamic countries, offering rewards for the capture of Osama bin Laden and his cronies. The restaurant itself is stunning; it is the work of one of the city's best young designers, Bára Skorpilová, the whole being slick and contemporary. The architect uses a mixture of media: wooden floors and slatted walls, wrought-iron partitions, plants, stone and glass all play their part. The menu is as eclectic as the building materials, part European, and part Asian, with a particular emphasis on fish. The food isn't stunningly original, but it is delicious and beautifully

presented, and there's a good selection of dishes and wines to choose from.

Food 8/9, Service, 8 Atmosphere 8/9

U Zlaté Studně, U Zlaté Studně 4, P1.
Tel: 257 533 322 www.zlatastudna.cz
Open: 7am–11pm daily   800kc

Part of the hotel of the same name, 'The Golden Well' offers a fantastic terrace restaurant looking out over Prague. The restaurant is spread over two levels. The downstairs area is decorated in a simple but modern style. Large windows supply a fabulous panorama over the city, and the furniture is contemporary, with clean wooden lines and crisp white tablecloths. Upstairs, the beautiful open terrace is fantastic for summer evenings or winter lunches, or even just for a drink to sip as you gaze out over the city. The menu is international with a leaning towards French cuisine, offering a delicious selection of fish, meat and game. U Zlaté Studně has an above-average wine list and it is gratifying to see proper care taken over its storage. Light jazz is piped out in the background, creating a relaxing and chilled atmosphere. Great for a romantic summer dinner as the sun goes down.

Food 8, Service 7, Atmosphere 9

drink...

The words 'Czech' and 'beer' are almost synonymous. This is the birthplace of Pilsner and the original home of Budweiser, as well as a range of fine lagers with unpronounceable names.

Pubs and bars are an integral part of local life. Pubs are predominantly the domain of the Czech man, and are often simple and rough, serving little more than a perfect pint of the local beer, occasionally accompanied by some fried cheese. Unwelcoming and slightly intimidating for women, Czech pubs are a law unto themselves, refusing to change their traditional ways.

Bars have come a long way in Prague owing to the influx of tourism over the last decade. Some are basic low-lit cellar affairs, while others are modern, sleek and elegant. The smarter bars are mainly found to the north of Old Town Square, in the so-called 'triangle of sin'. They have enough cocktail tomes, elegant ice maidens and businessmen to make you believe that you never left Soho, but of course, all at Prague prices. Mixed in the student-orientated bars offer plastic glasses, cheap and badly mixed cocktails and buzzing atmospheres.

SoNa, to the south of the National Theatre, is home to young, aspiring and alternative Czechs. Less pretentious than the Old Town, the atmosphere is more convivial and the drinks cheaper. Instead of flashy neon, stainless steel and pine furniture, SoNa provides updated examples of traditional Czech hostelries – each different from the other – but here you sit and chat with a drink instead of standing and posing.

A third area to be aware of is Mala Straná, the district under the Castle on the west bank of the Vltava. Here the bars obviously attract more tourists who are either staying in the area or popping in for a quiet early evening drink. Outstanding are Bazaar, with its fantastic terrace adorned by the beautiful crowd, while St Nicholas' Café entertains the more sophisticated local professionals drawn from the surrounding embassies.

Cafés play just as an important role in the social drinking scene of Prague as the bars do. Such places as Café-Café are open late into the night and are populated by the young and glamorous. Some restaurants also have bars attached where it is worth whiling away time pre- or post-dinner: Hergetova Cihelná and Square are great examples of these.

In the centre there will always be bars that are busy, but slightly away from the tourist hordes attendance will fluctuate according to the day of the week. Don't expect anything to be truly cutting-edge; this is Prague and it is a couple of years behind the bar scenes of London, Paris and New York – but then again that's part of the charm.

Few bars have door policies and you certainly won't end up paying to get in. Some bars, especially the smarter ones, now actively discourage or prohibit large groups of men from entering, which means marauding stag parties will be kept at bay.

Drinks are cheap: in a local pub a half litre of beer should cost about 25kc (50p) while in the bigger bars in town you can expect to pay about 40–50kc (80p–£1); and even more if you're in a tourist bar on Old Town Square. While local wine can be delicious, it can also be vinegar. It can be had remarkably cheaply, so don't be afraid to try. Some of the reds are particularly good. Cocktails are normally sold at around 100kc (£2), although naturally prices will vary according to the strength of cocktail and appeal of the location.

Alcohol Bar, Dušní 6, P1.

Tel: 224 811 744 www.alcoholbar.cz

Open: 7pm–2am daily

Just behind Old Town Square, in the chic district of Josefov, is one of the city's less originally named, yet more exclusive bars. A warm and intimate basement with a long wooden bar, Alcohol houses one of the most impressive whisky selections in Prague. There is a full range of cocktails, as well as a well-stocked *humidor*. The atmosphere is old-fashioned – more gentleman's club than Czech pub – and, as is typical for the area, prices are high, which means that the majority of the clientele will be businessmen, tourists and successful locals. Simple bar snacks are served if you get peckish as the night goes on. We found it really very civilized, but if you hate cigar smoke it might not be your kind of place.

Banana Café, Štupartská 9, P1.

Tel: 222 324 801 www.laprovence.cz

Open: 11am–2am daily

Recently taken over, extended and brought into the 'noughties' by the team behind über-restaurant Kampa Park and Hergetova Cihelná, Banana is about to regain its old place among the city's more fashionable set. A few steps from perennial US college-student hang-outs Chateau and Marquis de Sade, the bar is in the centre of late-night Old Town decadence. It was once famous for its Wednesday night transvestite shows and cheap drinks, but now the emphasis has shifted to expertly mixed drinks and society gossip. The bar has undergone a design transformation with a large metal elephant's head overseeing all the proceedings, while trappings that could have come straight off the banana boat dominate the walls. Whether the go-go dancers who performed nightly are going to continue remains an unanswered question. However, what is sure is that the Banana Café is back; it will no longer have to dwell on past reputation, because the party is about to get started again.

● **Bazaar, Nerudova 40, P1.**
Tel: 257 535 050 www.restaurantbazaar.cz
Open: 6pm–2am daily

Once fêted by *Tatler* as the place in Prague, Bazaar still manages to attract the higher echelons of Prague society and Europe's hippest tourists. In the summer months, a rooftop garden terrace is open overlooking the city, creating a heady cocktail of potent drinks and eye-popping views. This is where the beautiful people congregate on a warm summer's evening to sip and chat. Inside, next to the restaurant, is another bar that offers near-horizontal lounging and hookah pipes mixed with club/lounge music for the colder autumnal evenings. Taken over, like the Banana Bar, by the Kampa group, it promises to combine fashion,

design and celebrity as it has in its other ventures. Doormen and women keep a watchful eye to keep the groups away and preserve the sophistication of the atmosphere.

Bombay Cocktail Bar, Dlouhá 13, P1.
Tel: 222 328 400
Open: 6pm–3am (4am Friday–Saturday) daily

One of the major cocktail players in the 'triangle of sin', Bombay has made significant strides in becoming more up-market in recent years. Gone is the drinks list plastered in brightly coloured crayon on the mirror behind the bar – instead more elegant cocktail menus have arrived. In fact, these are almost a book in themselves, with several pages dedicated to each base spirit alone; the selection is not uninspiring but neither does it

really try and break any new ground, sticking to old favourites or variations on them. Bombay attracts a slightly less sophisticated audience than neighbouring Tretters or Ocean Drive, but then again they don't tend to mix their cocktails with cheesy dance music and flashing lights. The foreign contingent seems to hunt in packs, and consequently it's a popular destination with stag, hen and college groups. At the weekend it definitely has a buzzing atmosphere, fuelled by alcohol and euro-pop.

Bugsy's, Pařižská 10, P1.
Tel: 222 329 943 www.bugsysbar.cz
Open: 7pm–2am daily

One of the *grandes dames* of Prague's burgeoning nightlife scene, and one of its three premier cocktail establishments, Bugsy's seems to have lost some of its legendary exclusivity as other nearby competitors open up. Recently renovated after near-total destruction in the 2002 floods, the small cellar bar has taken a leap forward in its décor, style and feel. The disproportionately long bar is home to more liquor than you'll see in a while, collated to create near perfect cocktails. The drinks list is fantastic: concoctions past, present and future all seem to make an appearance, enticing you to stay at the bar for that little bit longer as you'll 'just need to try that one…'. Its location is supreme, a few steps from the seriously expensive and fashionable shops of Pařižská; the smart and the fashionable come for

an early evening aperitif, while later on businessmen, elegant locals and affluent tourists sup to the sounds of live music. Luckily they don't allow it to get too full, but it will always be busy.

Chateau, Jakubská 2, P1.
Tel: 222 326 242
Open: noon–5am daily

Chateau is *the* American college hang-out in Prague and guaranteed to be busy every night of the week. Inside typical Prague – deep-red walls, low lights, large mirrors and high ceilings – is mixed with loud music, cheap drinks and all manner of piercings. Don't expect it to be civilized, but it is a great place to go and meet people. It appeals hugely to college students and young ex-pats who hang around outside smoking dope or talking loudly at each other. ('Well, like, it is the thing to do, like, man.') There is a decent selection of cocktails plastered all over the mirrors behind one of the bars. Chateau has just opened a new basement club that has lived up to the reputation of the bar – brash and drunken, full of attitude and opinions. An ex-pat establishment, specializing in college kids and not for the faint-hearted.

Cheers, Kremencova 17, P1.
Tel: 776 390 292 www.h2ocafe.cz
Open: 5pm–2am daily

Ignore the unoriginal name and relish the distinctly cool orange and black interior of this new bar in the centre of SoNa on the site of the old Red Room. Heavily varnished wooden benches, tables and chairs stand out against the luminosity of the orange walls. The bar seems to have a double focus, attending to the needs of the cocktail-drinking urbanites that frequent SoNa as a whole, as well as the more edgy cooler group who sip neat whisky and talk quietly to the bar staff. The music system, totally at the mercy of the bar staff, churns out a heady mix of dance, lounge music and heavy rock, depending on the mood of the barman that night – it can get quite intense. The clientele is young and switched on, interested more in a drink and chat than meeting anyone else.

Duende, Karolíny Světlé 30, P1.
Tel: 222 221 255 www.duende.cz
Open: 11am–1am Monday–Saturday; 5pm–1am Sunday

Located on an unassuming, yet strangely fashionable street running parallel to the river, Duende's façade gives little away and the inside is equally unostentatious, yet this is a great place to come for a couple of late-night drinks. The friendly staff happily pour drinks and chat to the clientele, who are a very eclectic bunch ranging from bohemians to tourists, and from minor celebs to businessmen, and it doesn't crowd out too badly. Duende is the definition of shabby-chic – the two rooms are simply furnished and decorated with a purposefully cluttered assortment of knick-knacks and posters. There is something here for everybody, and by remaining unpretentious it has managed to draw a sophisticated crowd, so expect chilled, laid-back music, long drinks and interesting conversation.

Inn Ox Bar, Carlo IV, Senovážné Náměstí 13, P1.
Tel: 224 593 090 www.boscolohotels.com
Open: 10am–2am daily

The bar at the Carlo IV is one of the most stylish and contemporary in Prague. Designed by Adam D. Tihany, it would grace the most stylish hotel in London, Paris or New York. The long, central bar dominates the room; finished in back-lit glass and steel it is extremely elegant and forms an illuminated centrepiece to this glamorous interior. Long white curtains flow over the windows

while groups of Prague's elite and the city's more glamorous visitors sip exquisitely prepared cocktails. There is a cigar bar on the other side of the lobby which is housed in the old vaults of the bank and exists as a separate entity. Dark and intimate, it is the perfect place for a romantic interlude or an after-dinner glass of brandy.

Joshua Tree, Na Příkopě 22, P1.
Tel: 221 451 271 www.joshuatree.cz
Open: 11am–3am daily

A new Irish bar in the heart of the city, but with the exception of the name (after the eponymous U2 album) and the menu, it is not obviously Irish and certainly not your traditional brawling bar. It occupies a vast underground cellar on two levels, secreted beneath one of the better shopping malls in the city. It is as close to the hipper pubs of London or Dublin as Prague gets, but whether that's a good thing or not is for you to judge. The rooms are cavernous, and the under-lit bar and spotlighted bottles help give it a modern if industrial feel. By far the largest bar

in the centre of the city, Joshua Tree aims to lure in the glamorous, young Czechs dining upstairs at Kogo (see page 87) as well as the more urbane ex-pat. Live Irish music is all part of the fun and at weekends bands keep over-excited punters dancing to old favourites as well as the ubiquitous U2 covers.

Kozička, Kozí 1, P1.
Tel: 224 818 308 www.kozicka.cz
Open: noon–4am daily

A typical Czech basement bar, playing host to some tourists and
ex-pats, but mostly to a crowd of rather hostile-looking locals.
Internally, it is not particularly impressive, nor does it really have
the atmosphere of anything other than a good neighbourhood
bar, despite being just off Old Town Square. Its brick walls and
wooden furniture underlie its simplicity and homely neighbourhood feel. It has the requisite pair of attractive Czech girls who
sit and pout in the corner of the room, expertly sidestepping the
advances of hopeful foreigners. The bar staff seem a touch xeno-
phobic and have little time for anyone who doesn't at least speak
a modicum of Czech. It is not as welcoming to tourists as many
other bars in the area, but if you can brave the frosty staff and
the mafia lookalikes, it's not too bad at all.

K.U. Café, Rytížská 13, P1.
Tel: 221 181 081
Open: 2pm–2am daily

K.U. Café (for 'Kent Universe Café') is one of Prague's hippest
bars of the moment. Tucked in between Old Town Square and
Wenceslas Square, it is right in the centre of it all. Designed
sleekly and extremely chicly for the Czech Republic, K.U. is *the*

place of the moment, populated by the young and the beautiful. The clientele, so I am assured, are drawn directly from the social pages and gossip sections of the press. The fine selection of cocktails, well proportioned and mixed, are conducive to a fine evening, as you and everyone around you unwind. You shouldn't have the problems getting in that you might in London: the door policy is fairly relaxed except when it gets too busy.

Legends, Týn 1, P1.
Tel: 224 895 404 www.legends.cz
Open: 10am–1am (4am Friday–Saturday) daily

This is *the* venue for watching sport – if there is an important football, rugby or boxing match happening, then it's guaranteed that this bar will be showing it, and they can show up to four matches simultaneously. The brick cellar bar is a long thin room

with rows of televisions along each wall and a large screen at one end. There are tables under the televisions, as well as a large central island you can sit around and watch several matches at the same time. You're unlikely to come across many locals here, as it's more of an ex-pat and tourist hang-out; and expect it to be loud, raucous and drunken, especially on big match days. They provide a decent selection of food and drinks to help sustain you through those emotionally charged games. If there isn't a big game on, it can be rather quiet.

M1, Masná 1, P1.
Tel: 221 874 256
Open: 6pm–4am daily

A relatively new bar in the middle of the 'triangle of sin', opened in the summer of 2002, M1 has a strong industrial feel with concrete floors and a metal bar, although the look is slightly softened by the red velvet banquettes running along the walls. There are small stainless-steel tables placed at regular intervals and the large mirrors at each end increase the feeling of space. During the week it is a great place to come and lounge and chat to the background beats of the DJs, and at weekends it's as busy as its British namesake on a bank-holiday weekend. Its residents are young and trendy Czechs and ex-pats, and generally M1 has a vibrant atmosphere. Grab a seat, some of which are on wheels – inciting juvenile behaviour – and enjoy first-class service from an

elegant, designer-clad blonde. Great to spend the night in, or come just for a couple of drinks *en route* to one of the city's finer clubs.

Marquis de Sade, Templová 8, P1.
Tel: 224 817 505
Open: 11am–2am daily

Once the largest brothel in Prague, Marquis de Sade is now a popular student hang-out. Don't be too put off – this is one of the most original and interesting bars in the city. Fantastically high ceilings, deep-red walls, large modern canvases, low-level lighting, simple wooden tables and chairs all add to the unique-ness of the bar. One can see how the brothel might have once worked; a balcony at one end is where the girls would have flaunted themselves to entice men to the upper floors. Today much of its original splendour has disappeared, and what remains is laid-back and shabby, and thus entirely suited to both the clientele and the atmosphere. A range of cocktails does little to dispel the student image, especially as they tend to be pretty poorly mixed. However, there is a definite bohemian edge to the place, with its dim lighting, hovering smoke level and decidedly

cool music, and an alternative video shop in the corner renting out cult classics helps set the tone. A great place to reminisce about what used to be, in a seedy young venue.

U Medvídků, Na Perštýně 7, P1.
Tel: 224 211 916 www.umedvidku.cz
Open: 4pm–3am daily

An old-fashioned Czech beer hall and pub in the centre of the town, U Medvídků hasn't yet been spoiled by the influx of tourists, although it has been known to cater for small tour groups, so disaster may loom. The pub is really quite small: a copper bar stands in the centre of the room, constructed from old brewing paraphernalia, with a small lounge area next door where locals watch football or ice hockey. More space is available in the larger beer hall next door, which serves up some decent traditional food alongside delicious Budvar. There is a garden at the rear, open during the summer, but it's tiny, enclosed and with no view. Upstairs is a little *pension*, which has retained as many of the original features as possible. The main attractions are the beer and the authentic Czech vibe. Good as a late night pit-stop on the way home from dinner or for a relaxing drink in the afternoon shade.

Ocean Drive, V Kolkovně 7, P1.
Tel: 224 819 089 www.tretters.cz
Open: 11am–2am daily

Tretters' younger sibling, Ocean Drive, has added some grown-up glamour to the 'triangle of sin'. An American-themed cocktail bar protected from the outside world by long, flowing white drapes and inside shrouded in intimacy and candlelight, it offers exclusive relaxation and networking for some of Prague's finest. Like its more famous neighbour, the emphasis is on style and sophistication – 30-something Czechs mingle, sipping potent and exotic cocktails, chatting above the low-level music. The walls sport pictures of carefree life on the coast, providing a perfect backdrop for girls and boys pouting at each other over martinis, hoping to find the elusive dream partner. Ocean Drive has built upon Tretters' reputation for providing an exclusive and deca-dent retreat for some of Prague's more affluent residents.

Od Soumraku Do Úsvitu, Týnská 19, P1.
Tel: 224 808 250
Open: 2pm–4am Monday–Friday; 6pm–4am Saturday–Sunday

In English, the name of this bar means 'From Dusk Til' Dawn', but film aficionados should not be put off – it is little like Tarantino's film, although some of its inhabitants are just as strange. Just off Old Town Square, it could be a great little bar, but currently seems to be overrun by the grunge fraternity: Americans with goatees, tattoos and piercings. Expect loud music, long baggy shorts and vacant stares from behind outlandish facial hair. It can scare the average customer off, instead favouring the mid-20s US and Czech crowd, who feel right at home. You could join the odd baffled tourist or two sitting quietly in the corner, but don't worry – the staff and clientele are all perfectly friendly and don't actually bite; instead they serve up a surprisingly good selection of cocktails. The décor has a minimalist industrial feel, with concrete walls and bar, and the back-lit bottles provide an eye-catching visual focus. It is simple and could be rather fashionable, stylish and successful.

Radegast, Templová 2, P1.
Tel: 222 328 069
Open: 11am–midnight daily

One of the old-fashioned Czech pubs in the centre of town that doesn't pander to the tourist trade. A long narrow room with tables and booths running down each wall draw you in, while the round vaulted ceiling and room proportions give you the impression of being seated in a barrel. Take a seat and get started on as much fine Radegast beer as you can manage; munch on traditional Czech food in the company of salt-of-the-earth Prague locals,

and you'll soon discover it's not just the British builder who likes to slope off early! It really is a no frills affair, wholesome and down-to-earth, consequently it's not as loud and noisy as some of the other beer halls, but just feels more genuine. There's no better place in the area for cheap beer and food.

St Nicholas' Café, Tržiště 10, P1.
Open: noon–midnight (3am Friday–Saturday) daily

One of the more relaxed places to come for an evening drink, St Nicholas' Café is home to a more sophisticated clientele, some of whom work in the embassies that surround the area, while others are too civilized to join the rest of the tourist horde. Its steep entrance steps and low-vaulted ceilings suggest just another cellar bar, but this place is different. Strategically placed lamps and funky music promote an ambience of calm and intimacy. This is a quintessential Prague bar/café, definitely the sort of place to come and chat and drink. The service is attentive and friendly, if a little slow, but then again spending time in St Nicholas' Café encourages slothfulness. One of the more refined places, great for a relaxing drink before heading across the street to U Malého Glena, the small and smoky jazz club.

Tom Tom Club, Dlouhá 46, P1.
Tel: 224 828 374 tomtomclub@volny.cz
Open: 10am–1am daily

A chilled, laid-back and dimly lit bar on the busy street of Dlouhá. The walls are painted in the traditional Czech blood-red and decorated with different and distinctive ornamentation, especially in the back room. The furniture is a variety of simple, wooden tables and chairs, all slightly different, shabbily creating an ambience of modern simplicity. Ornate chandeliers hang from the ceiling, whil strategically placed lamps help to create a comfortable, low-lit atmosphere. The clientele are young and trendy Czechs, who come to drink, chat and smoke rather than shout, pose and jostle for position. This is a relaxed counterpoint to many of the loud and bustling bars in the area, and ideal for a drink before you head off to a gig or a night at the Roxy. Tom Tom is great for a first-date drink and a quiet evening out, beyond the reach of the tourists who normally inhabit the area.

Tretters, V Kolkovně 3, P1.
Tel: 224 811 165 www.tretters.cz
Open: 7pm–3am daily

The sophisticated hang-out for Prague's exclusive and wannabe glam set. The bar is bursting with the suited and booted, entertaining a beautiful trophy girlfriend or in pursuit of the elegant girls who perch at the edge of the bar. An extensive list of cocktails is contained within a hard-backed tome found on the bar, enough to tempt you to spend the entire weekend sifting through its contents. The bar staff are smart and efficient, and do amazingly well to cope with the constant demands at peak peri-

ods, as it is difficult to churn out such delicately made drinks. A fantastic place to seek your dream long-limbed model, or just sit and watch the competition make their attempts; our survey suggests you will need to be either well dressed or rich before they take pay any attention to you. Always popular and busy, Tretters is a great place to people-watch and mingle with the hip and beautiful.

Ultramarin, Ostrovní 32, P1.
Tel: 224 932 249 www.ultramarin.cz
Open: 11am–4am daily

A grill bar cum music club on the edge of SoNa which has recently been extended to cope with its popularity. (In Prague, if there aren't seats available, customers just tend to leave – they don't stand around.) Ultramarin is not as modern or chic as

some as the other bars/restaurants in the area but it has an excellent, buzzing vibe, and is one of the few places that is always full. Frequented by a mainly young Czech crowd, the menu offers up some tasty food well into the early hours. Found on a small street off the tourist trail, it is part of the Elite Hotel.

Downstairs is a basement club that serves more as an extension to the bar than a nightclub. Its red-bricked, high ceilings provide a great backdrop for relaxed late-night drinking. Distinctly chilled, it's not the sort of place to chat up or be chatted up, but instead a great bar to go and eat, drink and chat the night away.

U Zlatého Stromu, Karlova 6, P1.
Tel 222 220 441
Open: 24 hours daily

In many ways the consummate bar: open 24 hours, with a dance floor, a relaxing drinking area and pole dancers downstairs. Located on the Royal Way, just a few yards from Charles Bridge, right on the tourist trail, inevitably it is full of foreigners who have stumbled in for some cheap nudity or dinner on the terrace outside. The 50kc entrance fee won't break the bank for a quick look, and if pole dancing is not your cup of tea, there is always the subterranean bar. Beware of the prices – the Czechs appear to pay a third of what you might for a glass of beer. It's all harmless and unthreatening, if slightly seedy, and offers a rather easy introduction to the 'darker side' for the uninitiated, if you haven't frequented such an establishment before.

Zvonařka, Šafaříkova 1, P2.
Tel: 224 251 990 www.zvonarka.cz
Open: 11am–2am (midnight Sunday) daily

A wannabe cool bar/restaurant in the heart of Vinohrady, Zvonařka is all about glass, steel, neon and wood combined to create a modern space with sleek and simple lines. There are separate bar, restaurant and lounge areas and a large outdoor terrace offering panoramic views over the city's southern reaches. It's known to host some of the best private parties in town, so if you're able to crash one consider yourself a legend; otherwise, they still have Prague's finest DJs spinning the decks at weekends. A good venue in which to catch young trendy Czechs and the funkier ex-pats doing what they do best. The restaurant is reasonable but its Mexican/Asian/Czech food is nothing to shout about. Nevertheless it's certainly worth a visit if you're staying in this part of town.

snack...

Café culture is an important part of Prague life. Cafés are places to meet, chat, eat and drink – especially for women. The traditional Czech pub, with its often drab, smoky surroundings, is a very masculine environment where few women feel comfortable, but cafés can provide a safe outlet for socializing without fear of being mauled by marauding stag parties.

There are two sorts of café in Prague: the smart and chic, and the traditional and cosy. The traditional cafés can be enshrouded in smoke, but serve decent, hearty food and glasses of local wine. Frequented by locals and the occasional more bohemian tourist, they are invariably welcoming and friendly, and provide a quiet and comfortable pit-stop – a tempting refuge from the cold outside.

Smarter cafés, such as Nostress and Café-Café, have emerged over the past five years and tend to draw in a more sophisticated crowd: glamorous locals, afflu- ent ex-pats and switched-on tourists come for the delicious food, calorie-laden cakes and proper coffee. Often lighter and airier than more traditional cafés, they serve salads and cappuccinos at a premium.

A couple of the cafés mentioned here serve delicious gourmet food but have

not been classified as restaurants because of their limited capacity: Café-Flambée, Sovový Mlýny and Clementinum are prime examples. Others such as Au Gourmand and La Dolce Vita specialize in incredibly fattening but delicious cakes and puddings.

One unusual phenomenon in Prague café culture is the prominence of the tea house, serving rare and delicate teas from around the world in peaceful and relaxing surroundings. Dobrá Čajovna and Dahab are interesting and ethnic, offering tranquillity, space and a fantastic range of teas.

Cafés are generally much cheaper than restaurants but a little more expensive than pubs. It is unusual to pay much more than 40kc for a glass of wine or beer and 120kc for a plate of food.

Au Gourmand, Dlouhá 10, P1.
Tel: 222 329 060
Open: 9am–7pm daily

A former butcher's shop behind Old Town Square, Au Gourmand has since been elegantly transformed into a French-style patisserie. It sells a stunning array of cakes, desserts and a selection of delicious tarts and sandwiches. The room, still tiled from its butcher-shop days, has two serving counters dishing up sweets and savouries respectively. Everything is incredibly clean and fresh, almost to the point of sterility. At the back is a second small room with leather banquettes where you can lounge and gorge yourself on the large slices of cake. A small deli section provides gourmet food and wine to take away. Great for a quick bite on the move or a cup of tea and something sticky.

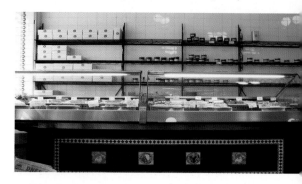

Café-Café, Rytířská 10, P1.
Tel: 224 210 597 www.cafe-cafe.cz
Open: 10am–midnight Monday–Friday;
11am–midnight Saturday–Sunday

On a warm sunny day, sit outside Café-Café sipping a coffee and watching the world go by – you won't regret it. In the evenings it is even better; it's currently one of *the* places to be seen. Situated between Wenceslas Square and Old Town Square, right in the centre of it all, it plays host to football stars, actresses and models as well as aspiring wannabes. Parisian chic is reflected in the large mirrors and windows, high ceilings and feeling of spaciousness. Even the service is a notch above cafés in the surrounding area, and although it is expensive by Czech standards, it is still cheaper than the tourist-traps on Old Town Square.

Café Carolina, Nerudova 44, P1.
Tel: 257 535 557 www.hotelneruda-praha.cz
Open: 7am–11pm daily

Attached to the chic, contemporary Hotel Neruda, this café serves industrially thick hot chocolate, in an elegant, modern room with large windows through which you can gaze at tourists struggling up the hill towards the castle. In fact, Café Carolina is a great place to stop and recharge the batteries with

a sugar rush, before you yourself embark on a tour of the Castle and its associated museums. Its clean lines and fashionable interior make a pleasant change from the tourist trap Czech restaurants that line the path of the Royal Way.

Café Erra, Konviktská 11, P1.
Tel: 224 895 788 www.erra.cz
Open: 10am–midnight daily

One of the many trendy, boho-chic cafés in Prague, based in a quiet street not far from the National Theatre. Erra is low-lit, with candles on every table and dim lamps strategically placed around the room; the café is below street-level anyway, so there is a constant darkness. The atmosphere is decidedly laid-back; people come here to eat, drink and chat in the latest designer clothes. The café is popular with the gay crowd, but it nevertheles welcomes everyone, and the music is funky and cool, played at just the right volume to allow conversation. The food is delicious and the portions are huge, so drop by and sample one of their mouth-watering sandwiches!

Café-Flambée, Husova 5, P1.
Tel: 224 401 236 www.flambee.cz
Open: 11am–11pm daily

An elegant, chic café in the heart of the Old Town, Café-Flambée is the sibling bistro to the expensive, formal restaurant of the same name. The crisp white tablecloths, comfy red chairs, pine floor and soft lighting grant it an exclusive and intimate atmosphere, while the strip mirrors on the wall and the stainless-steel bar lend it an air of modern sophistication. The innovative menu is divided into contemporary Czech food, a vegetarian selection and modern world cuisine, all complemented by a delicious dessert menu and cooked to perfection. Café-Flambée is a very select place, catering to a clientele in search of a more discerning venue, as well as providing a good alternative to the restaurant downstairs if it's fully booked.

Café Indigo, Platnéřská 11, P1.
Tel: 0602 789 443
Open: 11am–midnight daily

Café Indigo is a large, industrial-looking space with huge windows which, rather disappointingly, look out over the back of the Klementinum. There is a real mix of styles. Simple French café-type wooden chairs tucked under stainless-steel tables are set against a large industrial steel bar that dominates one side of the room, while strange sculptures and photographs decorate the corners and the walls. It's avant-garde for Prague, but in its interior you can discern elements of the design fashions of the last 30 years. The clientele seems to be made up of local Czechs, students and the odd bemused tourist who has strayed from the beaten track. Indigo's food is rather basic and predictable, but this is nevertheless a good spot to sit with a glass of red wine (and a pack of cigarettes, if you are so inclined), and blend into a new generation of Czech culture.

Café Louvre, Národní třída 20, P1.
Tel: 224 930 949 www.kavarny.cz/louvre
Open: 8am–11.30pm daily

Once you've penetrated the rather imposing and disconcerting entranceway and climbed to the first floor, you'll emerge into a set of warm café rooms. Café Louvre is perfect for those seeking solace from the cold in the winter and heat of the summer months. The rooms have high ceilings with impressive Art Deco chandeliers, while the walls are decorated with large posters and prints from a bygone era. It is mostly patronized by locals – small groups of women gather to chat over a coffee and a cake. The café offers a range of breakfasts according to nationality, and the

Czech version consists of garlic soup and beer. Now, you have to be quite dedicated for that!

Café Montmartre, Řetězová 7, P1.
Tel: 222 221 143
Open: 10am–6pm daily

A small, battered café with a cheery atmosphere, Café Montmartre is just a few steps off the tourist track. It has a worn, almost shabby appearance, as if all the furniture has been pulled straight out of a down-market antiques shop. However, underneath its barrel-vaulted, painted ceiling, the rooms are enlivened by a sleek clientele. There are three rooms, all furnished with wooden benches and old sofas parked on the tiled floors. Montmartre is all about drinking and chatting; its long bar and laid-back service provide an ideal backdrop for an eclectic assortment of people nattering over a coffee or glass of wine.

Café Slavia, Smetanovo nábřeži 2, P1.
Tel: 224 218 493
Open: 9am–midnight daily

This large café on the river bank is an old Prague institution. Situated next to the National Theatre, it was where plays were written and political debate nurtured. Café Slavia was refurbished a couple of years ago into the splendid Art Deco space it once was, with comfortable seating and large windows that boast super views up to the castle and Charles Bridge. It's great if you can get a seat by one of them, but you'll need to be alert to grab one. Slavia constantly manages to attract customers – normally tourists drawn by guidebook recommendations – and the prices reflect that. The menu isn't very exciting, but the café offers a pleasant enough ambience and is good for a coffee while you watch life – and the river – flow by.

Caffé Nuovo, Staroméstské námestí 5, P1.
Tel: 224 810 512
Open: 8am–midnight daily

A smart, contemporary café on Old Town Square, Caffé Nuovo makes a change from the tourist leviathans on the opposite side, but what you lose in view, you make up for in tranquillity and service. You won't find drunken English men or overloud American tourists here, but instead a more sophisticated and mature clientele. Nuovo's prices are much the same as the other cafés in the square, but instead of watery goulash there are decent sandwiches, salads, starters and a rampant selection of desserts on offer. Inside, the lines are crisp and the lighting subtle, accentuating the modern architecture of the whole. Wander up to the upstairs gallery, if the downstairs is full, for a little more peace and quiet. It is the sibling café to Dolce Vita and similar in décor and food. It makes a great pit-stop for a mid-morning or late afternoon snack.

Clementinum, Platnérská 9, P1.
Tel: 224 813 892 www.restaurant-clementinum.cz
Open: 11am–11pm daily

One of three decent cafés on this street, and next door to Café Indigo, Clementinum undoubtedly serves the best food of the three – although it is more of a place to have a meal than just drop in for a coffee. The café's contemporary design and feeling of airiness are provided by the stainless-steel bar and large windows looking onto the street. The staff are friendly, speak good English and are genuinely attentive. The food, a mix of Czech and international fare, is what you might expect from a stylish café but with a few unusual surprises, such as the wild boar chops. The clientele comprise discerning tourists rather than tour groups or students. The food is great value, making this a good spot for lunch.

Cukr Káva Limonáda, Lázeňská 7, P1.
Tel: 257 530 628
Open: 8am–11pm daily

A spankingly new café with chic décor, Cukr Kava is on a side
street just a minute's walk from Charles Bridge. The light wood-
en floors, dark walls and florally painted wooden beams all make
a refreshing change from some of the dingy cellar bars in this
part of Mala Straná. Relax with a fine selection of teas and drinks
and if you feel that you've earned it tuck into any number of
devilishly sweet, sin-inducing cream cakes. An extensive menu
consisting of crêpes, sandwiches, salads and breakfasts are as
good as they sound. Unobtrusive music helps to support the
really fresh and stylish atmosphere. Worth a visit to experience a
more up-to-date approach to café culture.

Dahab, Dlouhá 33, P1.
Tel: 224 827 375 www.dahab.cz
Open: noon–1am daily

Without doubt one of the funkiest places in town, Dahab is a
Moroccan tearoom, with a sedate, laid-back atmosphere. It is the
essence of what an Arab tearoom should be: pink vaulting sup-
ports a sky-blue ceiling, mosaic counters hide Arabian delicacies
and waiters scurry about with hookah pipes, while chilled music

adds an extra touch of serenity to what is already one of the most tranquil venues in Prague. Persian carpets and cushions set in front of traditional tables accommodate a mixture of Czech old hands, young ex-pats and the occasional tourist. A Lebanese menu offers a choice of savouries, starters and mezze, plus a wide selection of teas, coffees and cocktails. Everything is reasonably priced and the food excellent, so you will just want to try everything on the menu. This is a great place to spend a wet and windy afternoon unwinding – if only it offered massages as well!

Dobrá Čajovna, Václavské námesti 14, P1.
Tel: 224 231 480 www.cajovna.com
Open: 11am–9.30pm Monday–Saturday; 2–9.30pm Sunday

Hidden in a little courtyard just off Wenceslas Square, this is one of the best tea houses in Prague. Don't be put off by its somewhat grotty exterior. Inside it is spotlessly clean, the dimly lit room dotted with people chatting away quietly or lost in their books. Ambient music washes over the inhabitants, creating a rather surreal setting when contrasted with the cacophony of the square outside. Mobile phones and smoking are banned to maintain the purity. The tea menu stretches on for an eternity and the choice is spectacular: teas from the Americas, Africa and the East; white teas, green teas, black teas, red teas... it takes quite a while to choose. A bell is used to summon the waiter and once your choice is made a couple of minutes later the

most fabulous tea arrives, complete with the appropriate pot. There is nothing substantial to eat, merely a few snacks. But you will find an eclectic mix of tea-swillers: students, businessfolk and tourists, who all come to savour the unpretentious buzz.

Dolce Vita, Siroká 15, P1.
Tel: 222 329 192
Open: 8am–midnight daily

A small, elegant café found just around the corner from the main designer shopping avenue of Pařížská. It styles itself as a gelateria/café/bar, with a tempting selection of calorie-laden cream cakes and cooling Italian ice cream. Large windows expose shoppers struggling under the weight of their Dunhill and Hermes bags while, inside, the fresh cream walls are decorated with black

and white photographs of times gone by. Small, white linen-cov-
ered tables and smart black wooden chairs play host to the
wealthy and weary. An upstairs gallery area, really a spill-over,
offers a space for a more intimate chat. Dolce Vita is ideal for a
break from the exertions of shopping – enjoy a cappuccino and a
slice of its rich and sumptuous chocolate cake.

Evropa Café, Václavské námesti 25, P1.
Tel: 224 228 117
Open: 9.30am–11pm daily

Evropa is a large, imposing, Art Nouveau haunt overlooking
Wenceslas Square. Its grand interior, hefty chandeliers and mirrors are packed full of original 19th-century features, especially
evident in the rich use of dark wood and marble. However, this

is a real tourist hang-out; in the summer, when the terrace is
open, expect to be surrounded by groups of English lads swilling
beers and leering at women, barely conscious of the fact that it's
only 11am. Inside is rather formal, with a less than stimulating,
extortionately expensive menu (for Prague). This is an up-market
alternative to many of the other cafés on the square, but it
remains popular as a spot for a cup of coffee and people-
watching. The serenely elegant Czech women out shopping will
certainly catch your eye.

Globe, Pstrossova 6, P1.

Tel: 224 934 203 www.globebookstore.cz
Open: 10am–midnight (1am Saturday–Sunday) daily

Globe relocated to this contemporary space in the fashionable area of SoNa in about 2000. It is part internet café, part bookstore, part café, and the hang-out of the American student fraternity in Prague. It provides a nerve-centre for students and ex-pats where they can feel at home among hotmail addresses and English language newspapers. Globe serves some decent food and strong coffee for you to enjoy while surfing the internet on your own laptop. The staff are very friendly – indeed, you might find yourself drawn into the convivial English-speaking vibe and settle in for a few cocktails. But it is basically a place to pick up information, check email, grab a new book and have a coffee.

Kavárna Imperial, Na Poříčí 15, P1.

Tel: 222 316 012 www.hotelimperial.cz
Open: 9am–1am daily

Imperial is a large, old-world café on an unexciting, downtown shopping thoroughfare, and is one of Prague's defining images of faded grandeur. High ceilings and large windows look out over the street, walls and columns are clad in porcelain tiles, and the ceiling is covered in a complex mosaic. Nowadays both the patrons and atmosphere are reminiscent of the Communist era:

simple furniture and food, subdued conversation and enough smoke to make a salmon feel expensive. The service is slow and the menu unappetizing, but it is cheap and worth a quick coffee just to see the room. Great for retreating from the cold into the warm fug of a charming and timeless piece of Prague.

Kavarná Obecní Dům, nám Republiky 5, P1.
Tel: 222 002 770 www.obecnidum.cz
Open: 11am–11pm daily

This huge Art Deco room replete with fantastic chandeliers and beautiful wall-mounted light brackets is the home to Prague's most ornate and opulent café and Pilsen restaurant. Large windows look out on to the square where tourists mill around and

costumed concert-ticket sellers bid for custom. In the summer, there is terrace seating outside to take full advantage of the Continental warmth. A basic and rather unexciting menu of typical café dishes (salads, sandwiches and desserts) is on offer. As you might expect, dining amid such elegant ambience has a price; on the other hand it is still cheaper than Prêt-à-Manger. The room, however, clinches it – it is just too stunning not to stop in for a quick glass of beer.

Nostress Café, Dusni 10, P1.
Tel: 222 317 007 www.nostress.cz
Open: 8am–11pm Monday–Friday; 10am–11pm Saturday–Sunday

Nostress is a contemporary, elegant and sophisticated café in the heart of the Old Town. Large windows throw light into the striking room, illuminating the up-market clientele who lounge on designer leather armchairs, lulled by the sound of the water sculptures and soft jazz music. The curios and sculptures dotted around are all for sale, making Nostress part café and part lifestyle shop. In the front is a more formal café/restaurant that serves a selection of world fusion dishes, where a terrace overlooking the little square is open in summer. This is a modern designer bar, where you can expect to be served by tall, blonde ice maidens dressed entirely in black. Great for a quiet drink at the end of the day.

Le Patio, Národní 22, P1.
Tel: 224 918 072 www.patium.com
Open: 8am–11pm Monday–Saturday; 11am–11pm Sunday

Le Patio offers an oasis of calm and tranquillity in the midst of the hustle and bustle of Národní. Large double doors open onto the street to welcome in an up-market local clientele, keen to rest their weary feet after a hard morning's shopping. Inside, the high-ceilinged room is bedecked with Arab lanterns gently swaying to the silent rhythm of the ceiling fans. The imported designer furniture and knick-knacks, which are all available to buy, add to the oriental feel, but if nothing here takes your fancy go to the large shop at the rear, which has a great selection of furniture and lifestyle products. Chilled ambient music distracts you from the trams rumbling past the window. The essentially French menu has a good selection of light meals, salads, comfort food and a few extra treats, just right for a break from shopping before… well, carrying on shopping.

Radost FX Café, Běleradská 120, P1.
Tel: 224 254 776 www.radostfx.cz
Open: 11am–5am daily

The Radost empire is legendary, not only in Prague but also across Europe – London's Ministry of Sound once rated it as one of the top 20 clubs in the world. The café section occupying a quarter of the building has long been a Prague institution for the young and style-conscious as an important meeting-place. The furniture is mock-classical with comfortable banquettes, wrought-iron chairs and distressed tables, while in the larger rooms at the rear one can lounge on deep sofas and chill to the music. Radost FX is unashamedly cool, and a long cocktail list ensures that it is a favourite after-work venue for chic Czechs; and once the club beneath is in full swing, it acts as a port of calm amid the night-time storm below. Always busy, it is also noted for its fine vegetarian fare. It continues to serve food until the smallest hours of the morning.

Sovový Mlýny, U Sovových Mlýnů, P1.
Tel: 257 535 900 www.sovovymlyny.com
Open: 9am–midnight daily

Located in the Kampa Museum of Modern Art, Sovový is an elegant and contemporary space. The café is split into two areas, with an outside terrace open in summer that enjoys splendid views over the Vltava towards the Old Town. The simple décor is dotted with small but interesting pictures and *objéts*, and provides the perfect backdrop for a rather sophisticated menu. The dishes, which display a modern approach to Czech cooking, are just the right size to ensure that you can still manage to walk around the museum after lunch. We found the food delicious, demonstrating a refreshing approach to local cuisine and tourist management; Sovový does what it feels is stylish without pandering to local 'authenticity'. Now, if only we understood the art in the galleries above....

Tulip Café, Opatovická 3, P1.
Tel: 224 930 019
Open: 9am–midnight daily

With its modern, retro style (cream leather banquettes and
amethyst walls), Tulip makes a great location for a light bite to
eat. The simple menu of salads, sandwiches and breakfasts can be
enjoyed under the watchful gaze of old Czech film posters. It's
also a good place to relax: chilled music gently soothes away the
excesses of the night before while you sip a very strong espres-
so. Since it's in SoNa, it is mostly populated by trendy Czechs
and ex-pat businessmen who come for the laid-back atmosphere
and service as well as the tasty snacks. In the evening it begins to
fill up with locals here for some quiet conversation over a couple of glasses of wine.

Velryba, Opatovická 24, P1.
Tel: 224 933 591
Open: 11am–midnight daily

This cellar bar is packed full of young Czechs, and both conversation and music are loud. The clientele appear trendy and intellectual, if not particularly elegant. The large windows in the main room look up to street level while a mirror behind the bar gives the café creates the illusion of greater space. There is a smaller, more intimate room to the rear that often hosts small exhibitions and gatherings. Velryba serves decent vegetarian and, in their words, 'rational' meals as well as an impressive array of drinks, especially whisky. Good for a modern Czech intellectual experience.

U Zeleného Čaje, Nerudova 19, P1.
Tel: 257 530 027
Open: 11am–10pm daily

This cosy tearoom provides a resting-place on the long, steep walk up the Royal Way towards the Castle. It serves a range of traditional and original brews, from Earl Grey to Mongolian Smoked. The warm and welcoming atmosphere is tinged with the pungent smell of jossticks. The décor is simple and uncluttered, and the staff friendly and helpful. U Zeleného is not quite as relaxed or chilled as other tearooms, but is instead rather more sophisticated. It doubles as a shop, where you can buy a range of different teas and the corresponding accessories. Great for a relaxing cup of tea on the way up or down the hill.

U Zlatého Soudku, Ostrovní 28, P1.
Tel: 224 933 463
Open: 11am–midnight daily

Soudku is a small and friendly cellar bar, seemingly out of place on the edge of trendy SoNa. This is authentic and old-fashioned Czech with a distinctly down-to-earth trade. The café is spread over two levels: upstairs has a compact open-plan bar, while downstairs provides more intimate booths. A basic selection of food is served: quintessentially Czech in style, huge portions – which are surprisingly good – arrive to help the booze down. A reasonable selection of drinks includes decent beer but distinctly average wine, as well as the ubiquitous Becherovka. Coming in from the cold into this warm, smoke-filled room, you can sense that this is one of the better authentic Czech cafés.

party...

Nightlife in Prague is fantastic fun – very safe and unthreatening. The majority of the most engaging places are found in the centre, while those that aren't are merely a short taxi-ride away. Nightclubs rarely charge entrance fees and if they do it's often a minimal amount (maybe a pound or two). Drinks will be more expensive than in bars and pubs, but only slightly so – it also depends on the venue. The Prague nightclub scene, like many other European cities, comes in many different guises; there are tacky clubs, tourist clubs, trendy clubs and specialist clubs.

In the city centre are the tourist clubs situated around Old Town Square, advertised by neon lights and full of foreigners. You're unlikely to find many Czechs here. Such clubs as Arena and Lavka typify this. For cheesy clubs, try La Fabrique or Solidní Nejistota. These tend to be filled with young office workers who want to spend their hard-earned crowns getting drunk and trying to pull. The emphasis is more on alcohol than on the music or drugs. Often filled with friendly and entertaining locals and ex-pats, these places are less likely to have a chip on their shoulder.

Then there are a couple of clubs in Prague that are distinctly cool, which means designer clothes and expensive attitudes. The music will often be more serious,

with an emphasis on cutting-edge beats and DJs. They are not the sort of places to come to drink and pull, but are more about posing and pouting. A need to be seen in these places is an attraction, as well as the escape they offer from the cattle-market alternatives. Radost FX and Mecca are the best of these.

Finally the specialist clubs will concentrate on a particular style; for example, Industry 55 concentrates primarily on hardcore dance and techno music – not a place to go for a good night out with friends. Akropolis, while not necessarily specialist, does host decent local and international bands, and along with Roxy is a good venue to go for live music.

A visit to a casino can make or break a great weekend; you either win enough money to clear the hotel bill, or end up losing the taxi fare to the airport the next day. Having said that, they are always great fun and provide interesting people-watching opportunities. The casinos in Prague may not be as opulent as elsewhere in the world, often catering to tourists rather than the high-rolling elite. But there is always an air of expectancy; inevitably one or two card counters hoard large piles of chips, smugly sitting among crestfallen punters clinging to their few remaining crowns.

Minimum bets are similar to England, while maximums are considerably less, whether it is in crowns or dollars. Prague is rapidly becoming a gambling junket destination, with gamblers from Greece, Turkey and the Middle East filling the casinos for days at a time, spending their hard-earned cash.

While most casinos don't charge an entrance fee they will require you to have a passport, even if you are not betting. Soft drinks are invariably free to all, with free beer and wine to players, and food is free if you become a high-roller. There are no restrictions on licensing and you are allowed to drink at the tables.

151

NIGHTCLUBS

Akropolis, Kubelíkova 27, P3.
Tel: 296 330 911 www.palacakropolis.cz
Open: 4pm–4am daily

A very local, Czech establishment. Upstairs, at street level, is a canteen-style restaurant serving decent food, and also a concert venue, which puts on more alternative gigs and sometimes international stars. In the basement is the club; here live DJs spin the decks every night in any number of styles, from funk to trance. There are two different areas: the smaller bar area plays a harder beats mix, while the larger area pushes out a more funk/reggae sound. The aroma of dope pervades throughout, reflecting another national Czech pastime. Its habitués are definitely a little younger than in the more sophisticated places in town, but unquestionably hip. The drinks are cheap and it's usually free to get in. Akropolis is a great neighbourhood club with a buzzing atmosphere, and while you're unlikely to be surrounded by beautiful Czech models, it's an interesting and alternative option.

Arena, Melantrichova 5, P1.
Tel: 224 212 573
Open: 9pm–late daily

Find an underground venue, add sparkly disco lights, loud, cheesy music, a bright neon entrance and *voilà*. A den of tourist-orientated sexual iniquity, girls dance in groups in the centre of the room like a flock of sheep, while the predatory wolves watch in anticipation from the shadows at the edge. As soon as one detaches herself from the main group, a silent watcher pounces. It is as if David Attenborough could narrate. It's packed full of schoolgirls on field trips to the city and a few Czech boys in search of easy pickings – they come, they drink, they kiss and they pass out. On a Monday it is rocking, on a Saturday you can barely breathe, but the music is as tacky as it comes. A great place to watch schoolkids gyrating to what you remember schoolkids gyrating to.

DeMínka Music Bar, Škrétova 1, P2.
Tel: 603 185 698 www.deminka.com
Open: 8pm–6am daily

The Czech club of the moment, packed nightly with an array of stunning girls and well-dressed men strutting, posing and pouting.

DeMinka is one of the few places in Prague where you might have to queue to get in. It's spread over two floors: an upstairs bar and balcony overlook a larger downstairs brick bar and dance-floor. Not particularly smart or chic, it nevertheless seems to attract the more beautiful elements of the Prague scene. The music is based on pop and chart music and the drinks are reasonable, so it all kicks into action downstairs. The clientele is almost exclusively Czech and its prettier members seem wary of foreigners (perhaps rightly so), but it's still great for a night out.

Duplex, Václavské náměstí 21, P1.
Tel: 257 535 050 www.duplexduplex.cz
Open: 11pm–3am (5am Friday–Saturday) daily

Located on the sixth floor of a building in the centre of Wenceslas Square, this rooftop club/bar and restaurant enjoys fantastic views of Prague and its majestic castle by night. The entranceway off the street is pretty anonymous, and a lift transports you up to the lobby. The club itself looks like a *Playboy* video, with industrial walkways and cages hanging over the dance-floor. The seats in the booths around the side face out through huge windows, letting you watch the hustle and bustle of the square below. Duplex attracts a strange mix: a high entrance fee and drinks prices are prohibitive to many normal Czechs, while business people and tourists take their place. This leads us to believe that some of the beautiful girls' presence may be financially motivated. The regular DJs play a mix of chart and

house music, while international DJs drop in from time to time to raise the tempo. The staff add to the 'eye candy', which is just as well, as they aren't there for their speed or friendliness.

La Fabrique, Uhelný trh 2, P1.
Tel: 224 233 137 www.lafabrique.cz
Open: 11am–3am daily

Just outside the main tourist area, this is another example of clubbing at its cheesiest. Located on a small square, La Fabrique descends into the bowels of the city: two floors beneath cellar-level you will find a bar and a dance area. The club downstairs is

nearly always packed, with an unexceptional house DJ playing a mixture of dance and pop tunes. The crowd consists of ex-pats and young Czech secretaries and students who come in search of one another. Upstairs is more relaxed; a section is dedicated as a restaurant and the service at the bar is generally quicker than downstairs. If you decide to explore the downstairs area, you will find the wall of heat from the dance-floor hits you as you descend. It's definitely not for the nervous, but if you want a great time and a genuine prospect of meeting some local Czechs, then this is the place to come.

Futurum, Zborovská 7, P5.
Tel: 257 328 571 www.musicbar.cz
Open: 8pm–3am daily

Found in Smíchov, on the west bank of the river, this place appeals to a younger, less sophisticated crowd. Futurum's underground complex of rooms includes a huge video screen and dance-floor, famous for Friday and Saturday night 1980s and '90s parties. Full of energy, this dark and dingy club pulls in secretaries and office workers from miles around. The Mediterranean décor, featuring terracotta walls and tiled floors, is mixed with some modern steel attachments. Not the classiest place in town but if you want to get away from the tourists and immerse yourself in more provincial Czech nightlife, then this is the place for you. There is no need to dress to impress – nothing really gets going until about midnight, and it's very cheap once you're in, since the drinks come at local prices.

Industry 55, Vinohradská 40, P2.
www.industry55.cz
Open: 10pm–6am (8am Friday–Saturday).
Closed Monday–Tuesday.

Czech techno at its finest, set in an industrial-style club a short taxi ride from the centre of town. Inside, it can be quite difficult to tell what it actually looks like because of the smog-like smoke they pump out. The room is decorated with peculiar drug-induced sculptures that hang from the walls and ceiling and provide a welcome relief from the stark concrete floors and metal bars. The real selling-point of the club is that if you are an all-

nighter it goes on until midday the next day, demand permitting. The music is the most hardcore that Prague has to offer, and European guest DJs make regular appearances, as does the occasional established name, but mostly it is home-grown talent that fires up the punters. The music is pretty good, if you like euphoric techno or trance mixed in with some high bpms. During the week it can be quiet, save for a die-hard few dancing around like lunatics, but at the weekend you are certain to find plenty of company.

Karlovy Lázně, Novotného Lávka, P1.
Tel: 222 220 502 www.karlovylazne.cz
Open: 9pm–5am daily

Located on a promontory into the Vltava, Karlovy Lázně styles itself as the largest club in Middle Europe. There are five floors packed full of the young, the sweaty and the style-conscious. It is crammed with wannabes strutting their stuff, the majority of which seem to be American college kids. Karlovy Lázně has a good mix of tourists and young Czechs who really should know better, but just can't resist. The age range is young with most still waiting to break into their 20, but with cheap drinks and five floors of music, fun is the order of the day. Each floor has a different genre playing, from techno to pop to rock. The drinks aren't expensive for somewhere quite so central (and you'll need them). Overall, numbers are on your side, and this is a pretty good place to go to if you are determined to drink yourself into oblivion and charm a young, impressionable American.

Klub Lávka, Novotného Lávka 1, P1.
Tel: 222 222 156 www.lavka.cz
Open: 10pm–4am daily

Lávka sits beside Karlovy Lázně, on the very edge of the river bank. Its large terrace has fantastic views up towards the Castle and over the looming Charles Bridge. If the largest club in Middle Europe next door caters for those with pretensions of greater things, then Lávka caters for those who know their place. And their place is wading through crowds of people to cross the dance-floor, guzzling an over-priced beer and surrounding themselves with pure kitsch. There is a fantastic terrace to

remind you where you are before you return to the melting-pot. Chart classics past and present play, while tourists dressed to pull pout over their drinks. If your idea of a good night out is shacking up with a young Scandinavian or an American, then this is your place. The only Czechs you will find here will probably expect their drinks, entry and everything else paid for. You have been warned, but it's still a cracking night out.

Lucerna Music Bar, Vodičkova 36, P1.
Tel: 224 217 108 www.musicbar.cz
Open: 8pm–3am daily

One of the best live venues in the city centre, Lucerna is housed in an old theatre which exudes a simple, basic charm. Spread over two floors at the entrance to a large shopping arcade, on a street leading from Wenceslas Square, it plays host to some decent bands, both domestic and international. Like its sister club Futurum, it hosts lively 1980s and '90s parties at the weekends, when local office workers don their glad rags and join the fray. The minimum has been spent on décor, so expect basic tables, school chairs and plastic beer mugs. It is cheap and cheerful, and caters to a young Czech market who don't object to a bit of gritty realism. There are bars on both floors with a stage dominating the ground floor, while upstairs is a little more relaxed. Great if an interesting band is playing or if you want to enjoy a frugal night out in the centre of town.

For the definitively cool; ice-blonde über-babes elegantly ignore
bumbling tourists, as the latest dance music is pumped through
the club. It's expensive by Prague standards, and designer clothing
and luxurious accessories prevail. The furniture and design of the
place are chic and individual, with a great lighting system, sleek
modern lines and large, comfortable chairs. The bar staff would
look equally at home on the pages of *Vogue* as they do serving
cocktails. The music is cutting-edge, hosting sophisticated domestic and international DJs. Mecca is a place to pose, pout and
people-watch. Open during the day as a café and restaurant, it's
also a good place to unwind after a hard night's exertion. It does
involve a short taxi ride, but it is worth the trip.

The best known of the city's clubs, once included by the Ministry
of Sound in their list of the top 20 clubs in the world – a fact of
which they are still justifiably proud. Radost is the epitome of
cool on the Prague scene, frequented by ex-pats, celebrities and

serious clubbers. A quiet, laid-back bar with large sofas and comfortable chairs, it is home to a covering of beautiful people, who are being served a great selection of cocktails by the stylish and laid-back staff. On a lower level a smallish dance-floor hosts top international DJs, while a pumped-up designer crowd dance the night away. You do see the occasional glo-stick and whistle, but normally a more sophisticated class of clubber prevails. If you get a little peckish the vegetarian café (see page 145) upstairs serves fantastic snacks into the early hours. It is *the* club to hang out in, and a place to surround yourself with glamorous A-listers.

Roxy, Dlouhá 33, P1.
Tel: 224 826 296 www.roxy.cz
Open: 10pm–4am daily

The equivalent to Radost for the alternative music scene in Prague. Roxy hosts bands and DJs of international acclaim in a rather dingy setting, only a couple of minutes from Old Town Square. Where Radost has zebra-skin sofas, expect benches and school assembly chairs; where Radost has martini glasses, expect plastic beakers. It might look and feel unprepossessing, but it does host some excellent nights. The music styles range from house to ska to rock, so don't expect Britney Spears. The drinks are cheap and there is an almost constant odour of spliff coming from various different areas of the room. It is both hectic and frenetic in parts, and chilled and relaxed in others. The main

room is a huge, double height auditorium, with a balcony above
that allows a less energetic involvement. Find out what's on
before you go, or you might be in for a bit of a surprise.

Solidní Nejistota, Pštrossova 21, P1.
Tel: 224 933 086 www.solidninejistota.cz
Open: 7pm–6am daily

The 'in' club at the moment for the late 20- and early 30-
somethings crowd. It's worth hooking up with a local to point
out the actors, models and sports stars that hang out in this
blood-red club. A large central bar dominates the room, but
don't expect getting drinks to be a swift experience; you can
spend a fair time trying to be served. Solidni is packed with stun-

ning women who seem happy to drink themselves into near oblivion, before hitting the handkerchief-sized dance-floor in their equally handkerchief-sized outfits to groove to the latest cheesy pop music. A grill bar serves good steaks, chicken and the like until 4am, which beats the hell out of a kebab. Although it has the reputation of being one of the most expensive clubs in town, it's still cheap by UK standards. If you like a less than serious clubbing experience, then this is the place for you. A great venue, great people and an all-round good night out.

JAZZ CLUBS

Czech jazz, although no longer at the cutting-edge of the European scene, has a history that stretches back to the end of World War II. There is a host of jazz clubs around the city that put on nightly programmes, some for the serious enthusiast and the big names while others entertain more contemporary exponents of the art.

Jazz played its part in the fight against Communism and, in the past, Fascism. Music is one medium that is very difficult to silence, especially jazz, because its free-form expression was used as a symbol of defiance. Today the anger has gone and what is left are fluid jazz musicians who deliver faultless performances in smoky clubs.

Jazz Club, Železná, U průhonu 3, P7.
Tel: 224 239 697 www.jazzclub.cz
Open: 7pm–midnight

Železná has just relocated from its original smoky cellar in the heart of the Old Town to a super-club mecca in the suburb of Holešovice. The management doesn't limit the performances to just jazz, but brings in funk, acid jazz and a whole range of other styles. Consequently, the club attracts a young, vibrant crowd, and the laid-back atmosphere permits conversation with your friends. This means that it is great for a night out, far preferable to sitting in silence, surrounded by aficionados. The sets start at 9pm and are over by 11, so try to get there reasonably early to

order a drink and find a seat – otherwise you are condemned to
standing in the doorway.

U Malého Glena, Karmelitská 23, P1.
Tel: 257 531 717 www.malyglen.cz
Open: 10am–2am daily

From the outside this looks like – and to all intents and purposes is – a typical Czech pub with a live music sign, conjuring up
images of bad tribute bands. But luckily this is not the case. The
club downstairs is a live music lounge that plays young Czech
jazz at its finest, bringing in established musicians as well as a
great deal of up-and-coming talent. The sound in the tiny vaulted
cellar is amazingly intense; the audience is so close to the musicians they can almost touch them. The room only holds 20-odd
people and can get hot and sweaty once the set gets going.
Talent scouts loiter at the bar in the outer room, jockeying to

sign up the bands. The drinks are cheap and the crowd full of passionate young Czechs and curious tourists. It's worth a visit, although perhaps the Sunday night free-for-all is best avoided.

Reduta, Národni 20, P1.
Tel: 224 912 246 www.redutajazzclub.cz
Open: 9pm–midnight daily

A traditional jazz club made famous by Bill Clinton, who played his saxophone with President Havel. A large room with long tables and little round sofas. The walls are covered with black and white photographs of jazz musicians through the ages. Some fantastic jazz is played here, but its atmosphere is slightly more formal than elsewhere. The audience tends to be a mix of tourists and some serious local experts, and what is slightly off-putting is the inevitable appearance of video cameras filming the set. Not a place to sit around and chat, but intended for quiet contemplation and enjoyment of the music. Drinks need to be bought from a bar in a small side room. Reduta is popular among hardcore jazz fans, but don't feel you have to sit out the whole show.

CASINOS

Ambassador Casino, Václavské náměstí 5, P1.
Tel: 224 193 681
Open: 24 hours daily

Located on the top floor of the Ambassador Hotel on Wenceslas Square, it is slap bang in the middle of things. This complex boasts a large hotel and a 'top class' lap-dancing bar, should you feel like immediately sharing your hard-gambled winnings. The casino is modern and clean, with a mixture of slot machines and gaming tables. There are four blackjack and roulette tables as well as a poker table; bets start at 25kc for roulette and 100kc for blackjack. Although it's not entirely obvious, soft drinks and beer are free for players; everything else you have to pay for. The 24-hour opening means that after everything else is closed you can still spend the last of your money. The Ambassador tends to be full of tourists, and attracts a pre- and post-lap-dancing stag crowd from downstairs.

Casino Palace Savarin, Na Příkopě 10, P1.
Tel: 224 221 636
Open: 1pm–4am daily

A grand, old-fashioned room with chandeliers, Savarin retains many of its original features. The service is extremely friendly, courteous, professional, and in no way threatening. The beautiful old Baroque building dates back to the mid-18th century, and its impressive entrance from the street heralds the sophistication found inside. The stuccoed and columned interior is packed full of glamour – even James Bond would be comfortable here. The casino has five blackjack and six roulette tables, a pontoon and a poker table, and bets range from 20kc to 30,000kc. A separate room for high rollers provides free food and drink, while us mere mortals receive free soft drinks, wine and beer if playing, and can have a good meal at the small restaurant. It's a favourite of the ex-pat community and, although central, it isn't packed with tourists or gambling junkets from abroad. Undoubtedly the most sophisticated casino in the city.

ADULT ENTERTAINMENT

One thing that Prague is famous – or infamous – for is its adult entertainment. Wherever you are in the world, sex sells and few places are as cheap as here. The smut is divided into two sections: lap dancing and brothels. Don't be confused by street salesmen offering you 'strip shows' as more often than not they will really be advertising brothels, where you can sleep with the girl you have just seen strip. There are very few genuine stripclubs. Goldfingers, below, is undoubtedly the best but it is more expensive than elsewhere.

Sex can be found almost anywhere at a price: in brothels, on the street and even in nightclubs. Brothels are the easiest and safest; with a range of girls and clean facilities upstairs, they will provide and insist on the use of condoms. Street girls can be found just off Wenceslas Square; for a minimal fee they will service your needs in the lavatories of local bars. A few nightclubs will have working girls in them; it may be difficult to tell who they are, but if you ask what they do, you'll soon find out. The fourth option is the internet: www.erotika.cz gives you a good selection of girls with prices and locations.

Be sure you know the exact cost of what you are letting yourself in for. Some clubs will charge minimum drinks bills, others will confuse you with menu prices. At weekends the city is full of marauding British stag parties; the strip-clubs and brothels will be packed with them and the whole scene becomes more than a little depressing.

Atlas, Ve Smečkách 31, P1.
Tel: 296 224 260 www.atlas-cabaret.cz
Open: 7pm–7am daily

A largish 'nightclub' just off Wenceslas Square that is not threatening nor out to swindle you. You will be given a drinks card on entry, but do not lose it or you will be charged an extortionate amount to leave the place. The girls are attractive and friendly, but if you do not feel the need to partake be aware that there are live strippers on stage and the occasional live sex show. The rates for full, private participation are roughly 2,500kc for half an hour and 3,500kc for an hour. Atlas does tend to get very busy at weekends, and seems to attract a lot of overweight, leering men.

Goldfingers, Václavské náměstí 5, P1.
Tel: 224 193 856
Open: 9pm–4am daily

Goldfingers is the smartest and best-groomed strip-club in town, and home to elegant, leggy supermodels. Dances cost 1,000kc, while a more private dance (touching allowed) costs 1,500kc. This is the full extent of the funny business, as extra curricular activities are not on the menu. It is expensive, and drinks and dances are pricey in comparison with other strip-joints or bars. At the entrance they charge a cover of 450kc, and there are worrying signs stating that they do not allow guns into the club. Nevertheless, Goldfingers is very professional and not at all in-your-face – a good, safe introduction to the underbelly of

Prague's porn. The only problem is that at the weekends the club
does tend to get packed full of drunken British stag parties.

K5, Korunní 5, P2.
Tel: 224 250 505 www.k5relax.com
Open: 4pm–4am daily

K5 is the undisputed king of 'nightclubs': clean, stylish and run
with the professionalism you would expect from a five-star
hotel. The building is furnished with a club, bar/restaurant, a
relaxation area featuring a sauna, steam room and professional
massage equipment and of course 15 individually themed rooms
in which to enjoy yourself. On arrival you can either sit in the
club and have a drink, where each table is kitted out with tablet
computers telling you which girls are working that night, and
what their interests and statistics are, or make a direct decision
about which girl you want to spend time with, thereby saving
yourself the 500kc entrance fee. The girls working here are stunning, intelligent and friendly and more importantly are under no
obligation to be here. To spend time with one of them costs
roughly 2,500kc for half an hour or 3,800kc for the full hour.
Everything is about service, and there is even a questionnaire to
fill in when you leave. Here you won't be ripped off; everything is
done straight down the line and you can quite happily pay by
credit card.

culture...

Undeniably one of the most beautiful cities in Europe, Prague is an architectural synthesis of elegance, beauty and history. The city's charm lies in its combination of different facets, where the whole is greater than the sum of its parts. Unlike Paris or Rome, there isn't a world-famous cultural museum or gallery for sight-seers to gravitate to automatically – where Paris has the Louvre and Rome has the Vatican, Prague has Charles Bridge and Old Town Square. In other words, one is not limited by the confines of a museum or gallery, for the charm and beauty of the city lies in its ambience. Prague is a city that is best enjoyed by wandering the streets, enjoying the magnificent architecture all around you and soaking up the rich atmosphere of history. This is not to say there aren't inter-esting churches, museums and palaces to visit; it's just that it does not have the same must-see cultural focal points that other cities have.

There are always obvious points of interest in a city, and listed below are some suggested sights for visitors to Prague with limited time at their disposal. Most of them involve sitting with a cup of coffee and gazing with awe at the splen-dour of the surroundings. Prague's charm lies in wandering the narrow streets, coming upon little squares, exploring its nooks and crannies, and then retreating to a neighbouring bar or café.

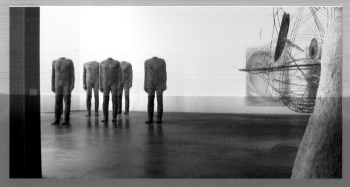

Prague is a world-renowned centre of arts and culture, famous for its music as well as its theatre and dance. There are three beautiful opera houses, which host magnificently staged performances of classic operas. The seats are incredibly cheap compared with London, and you are seated closer to the action. We highly recommend going to a performance – there are often Saturday afternoon matinees – and since all the classics are staged it could prove a good introduction to opera.

Most of the plays that are put on are in Czech, but some theatres provide simultaneous headphone translations to help you keep track of the plot. Black light theatre is another particular Czech favourite. This involves luminous paint/suits, ultraviolet lights and almost total darkness, allowing shapes to float across the stage, appearing almost weightless. Other forms of theatrical entertainment include a marionette version of *Don Giovanni*, a must for all opera lovers!

Every night a medley of concerts for which Prague is renowned is performed across the city, often in stunning surroundings. These are either specifically designed concert venues, such as the Dvorak and Smetana concert halls, or smaller churches that are architectural gems. The standard of music is high, with pieces drawn from all the major composers but with an obvious preference for the Czech greats – Dvorak and Smetana. It is a wonderfully civilized way to spend an afternoon and evening. And what could be more beautiful than listening to a string quartet in a candlelit baroque church?

SIGHTSEEING

Charles Bridge (Karlův Most), P1.

The large Gothic bridge that straddles the Vltava is a testament
to medieval engineering and was completed at the end of the
14th century. The statues were added in the late 17th and early
18th centuries. The Gothic towers at either end, built at the end
of the 12th and 14th century respectively, are home to some
ornate sculpture work. The bridge is lined with street vendors
hawking watercolours and photographs of Prague, caricaturists
and portraitists, and the occasional busking jazz quartet. The
bridge is often packed and can be tricky to push across at times,
which begins to get rather frustrating.

Kampa Museum, U Sovových Mlýnů 2, P1.
Tel: 257 286 147 www.museumkampa.cz
Open: 10am–6pm daily

The Kampa Museum is situated on the river bank overlooking
the Old Town, the Charles Bridge and the National Theatre.
Housed in an old mill that dates back to the 14th century, the
museum was opened in 2003, a year later than planned because
of the floods. The renovation has created a wonderful modern
space in which the best of Czech modern art is displayed. A per-
manent collection includes František Kupka and Otto Gutfreund

as well as prominent Central European artists, and temporary exhibitions take place. Apart from the beautiful architecture and thought-provoking art, the Kampa Museum offers a delicious and tempting café, Sovový Mlýny, where you can rest your feet and mind.

● **Mucha Museum, Panská 7, P1.**
Tel: 221 451 333
Open: 10am–6pm daily

The Czech Republic's favourite artist-son, Alphonse Mucha (1860–1939) was one of the most celebrated artists of the Art Nouveau period. He moved to Paris towards the end of the 19th century, where he spent time on individual commissions and designing advertising posters and shop façades. The Mucha Museum, a celebration of his art and life, is housed in the lavish Kaunický Palace. The gallery space is on the ground floor with

the works hung under the low-vaulted ceiling. The simple wooden floors and plain white walls all show off the splendidly colourful pieces to perfection – against the white backdrop the intricacies of the details really become obvious. This is one of the most popular museums in town, but it's worth a visit to understand the undercurrents of the Art Nouveau movement.

Náměstí Republiky, P1.

Not the most beautiful of squares in Prague, but it's home to two of Prague's most outstanding buildings. The Municipal House is one of the finest examples of Art Nouveau architecture in the country, if not Europe. The building holds several concert halls, salons, reception halls, restaurants and cafés. The architecture is decidedly opulent, the interiors are sumptuous and the ornamentation extravagant. Next to it is the markedly contrasting Powder Tower, one of the city's best-known landmarks, built at the end of the 15th century to form part of the Old Town's defences.

Old Town Square (Staroměstské náměstí), P1.

Old Town Square is seen by many as the focal point to the city. It's a beautiful film set of a square, surrounded by elegant buildings of different periods, in effect summing up the history of Prague. There is the fairy-tale Gothic Týn church, which looks as if it provided the inspiration for Disneyland. The Astronomical Clock draws crowds of tourists every hour to see the figures emerge, bow to the crowd and perform a medieval morality play, while they totally fail to comprehend dials and intricacies of the clock face below. The 14th-century Old Town Hall next to the clock has a tall, thin tower to climb; from the top one can admire the perfect panoramic vistas over the city.

Prague Castle (Pražský Hrad), P1.

Prague Castle rises over the district of Mala Straná, imposing itself on the skyline of the city. It is a steep walk to the top, but worth it for the views and the architecture that comprises the many different aspects of the Castle complex. Work first started on the Castle at the end of the 9th century and it has steadily expanded and grown into the edifice that it is today. St Vitus's Cathedral takes centre stage, with its fantastic Gothic façade standing in the middle of the grounds. Today the Castle is a

miniature town in itself, with churches, art galleries, the presidential palace and the heart of the government. The main art gallery holds some important works of art, particularly from the Renaissance and Baroque periods.

Royal Way, P1.

The Royal Way is the path that runs from Námestí Republiky to Old Town Square and up to the castle, crossing the Charles Bridge on the way. It winds through the narrow cobbled streets of the Old Town towards the river and then rises up the hill on the other side, past the grand St Nicholas' Church to the entrance to the castle. The streets are lined with shops packed to the gunnels with tourist tack: Prague Drinking Team T-shirts, models of houses, cheap glassware, hideous dolls and more souvenirs than you can shake a stick at. It is a beautiful route, nevertheless, surrounded by medieval and Baroque architecture, but it's absolutely packed full of tour groups, so if you want to dodge the crowds your best bet is late at night or early in the morning. Otherwise expect to be jostled through the streets.

Tourist Information Centre, Celetná 14, P1.
Tel: 224 491 764 www.aroundprague.cz
Open: 9am–8pm daily

Tourist information centres are the best place to find a private guide to take small, individual groups. Otherwise you can enrol in one of the many walking groups; pamphlets can be found in any of the tourist centres. You will probably find yourself in a group with complete strangers, following a guide holding an umbrella aloft. Prices are reasonable, and tend to be 300kc for a 2-hour tour. Wear some sensible shoes!

● **Wenceslas Square (Vaclavske náměstí), P1.**

The main square in the city centre has little of cultural interest except a few fine examples of Art Nouveau buildings. At the southern end, close to the State Opera House, is the National Museum, which dominates the main vista of the square. This houses a collection of stuffed animals and anthropological pieces, an inferior version of the Natural History Museum in London. Stroll around the square and have a drink in one of the many cafés around the edge, particularly the Evropa Café.

OPERA

● **Národní divadlo, Národní 2, P1.**
Tel: 224 913 437 www.narodni-divadlo.cz

The National Theatre, opened in 1881, is located on the river bank and forms part of the fantastic frontage that symbolizes the city. Its gold roof catches the sun, particularly in the evening, and can be seen from miles around. Internally it is similar to the

Estates Theatre with a sumptuous red and gold interior spread over four levels. Tickets can be purchased from the box office around the corner or on the evening of the performance from the foyer, as well as online. The programme is a mixed rotation of opera, ballet and theatre, which requires intense daily set changes. Some advance research is recommended.

Státní Opera Praha, Wilsonova 4, P2.
Tel: 224 227 693 www.opera.cz

The State Opera House is to be found at the top end of Wenceslas Square, close to the National Museum. Internally similar to the other two, it has lavish gold and red furnishings and ornate baroque swirls. Operas are staged every day, the majority Italian, with Verdi a firm favourite. Occasionally they add a little variety with a smattering of German and Russian composers. It is a little walk from the very centre but well worth combining

with a trip to the Zahrada v Opeře, one of Prague's finest restaurants, found in the same building complex. The box office is on the left, and tickets are available from the foyer as well on the evening of the performance.

Stavovské divadlo, Ovocný třída 6, P1.
Tel: 224 215 001 www.opera.cz

The Estates Theatre is most famous for hosting the world première of Mozart's *Don Giovanni*, conducted by the man himself. Its elegant façade forms the backdrop to Rytířská Street, with its classical columns and ornate pediments. Inside, the blue and gold interior is stunning and relatively small, so the performance seems far more intimate. It is like going back in time; if only everyone still attended in evening dress! Events alternate between theatre and opera, the latter inevitably featuring Mozart. Tickets can be bought at the entrance for forthcoming performances or for that night, or from the National Theatre box office on Národní. If you can, book up before you leave, and it is well worth getting a box.

CONCERTS

Klementinum, Karlova, P1.
Tel: 221 663 200

The Chapel of Mirrors in this church in the centre of the Old

Town has arguably the best acoustics in town for a church. The small and intimate space holds up to 100 people, who sit surrounded by fantastic gold Baroque ornamentation with a plethora of mirrors that reflect the candlelight. The music is eclectic, ranging from chamber music to Dvorak.

Prague Castle, P1.
Tel: 224 373 368 www.hrad.cz

If you can find tickets to an event here, it is well worth snapping them up, particularly those for the one-off spectaculars (see the website for advance notice of these, and bookings). Chorales and symphonies are sometimes held in the neo-Gothic splendour of St Vitus's Cathedral or the Spanish Hall.

Rudolfinium, náměstí Jana Palacha, P1.
Tel: 224 893 352 www.czechphilharmonic.cz

An immense neo-Renaissance building on the bank of the Vltava, the Rudolfinium is home to the Czech Philharmonic Orchestra. The roof of the building is rimmed with statues of famous composers. When the Germans rolled into Prague in 1938 they were aware that Mendelssohn, a Jewish composer, was depicted. Unable to discover from the records which statue represented Mendelssohn, they decided to look for the one with the biggest nose and destroy it. They duly destroyed the statue with the largest nose, only to discover, ironically, that it was the famous German composer Wagner. The CPO perform in the main Dvořák Hall, which seats 1,200, while the smaller Little Hall is more suited to chamber music. Restored comprehensively in the 1990s, it now contains a rather good, relaxed café.

St Nicholas Church, Staroméstské náměstí, P1.

In Old Town Square, this small church has nightly recitals that normally draw in a packed crowd of tourists, hell bent on a little culture and refined music. Completed in 1737, its splendid Baroque interior is a combination of ornate architecture and stuccowork. The acoustics are better suited to a booming organ than opposed to a haunting violin.

Smetana Hall, Náměstí Republiky 5, P1.
www.obecnidum.cz

Housed in the Municipal House, the Smetana Hall occupies the central section of the building and is home to the Prague Symphony Orchestra. There are three other smaller halls in the building, but the main Smetana Hall can hold almost 1,100 people, so the chances are you will find a spare seat. Keep an eye out for the people in costume outside, who will sell you tickets and are good source of information about what's on when. However, website has the best information about the larger upcoming concerts, especially those of the PSO.

CINEMA

Praha 1 and 2, Vaclavske náměstí 17, P1.
Tel: 222 245 881

This large cinema in the centre of Wenceslas Square shows a comprehensive selection of up-to-date and classic films, shown at a variety of different times, which make it quite difficult to predict what's on when. Most English and American films are in English with Czech subtitles, with the exception of children's films. Times and films can be found in the weekly English language newspaper, *The Prague Post*.

Slovansky Dům, Na Příkopě, P1.
Tel: 221 451 214 www.slovanskydum.com

This is part of the new shopping and entertainment centre on this busy shopping street, which has 10 screens showing a mixture of international and domestic films. It's very comfortable and reasonably priced, and you can grab a bite to eat at nearby Kogo, or a drink at the Joshua Tree beneath.

shop...

Every city in the world specializes in a particular product, and Prague is internationally renowned for its glass. Wherever you go in the centre of town there are glass shops selling pieces that range from the highest quality to cheap, often hideous tack. Much of the glass will be very ornate, and maybe too much so for some people's sensibilities. Good-quality glassware is cheaper than in the UK but getting it back intact presents a challenge. There are a couple of galleries that sell interesting glass art of a high standard, such as the Pyramid Gallery on Narodní.

There are various other products that are fairly ubiquitous around town: marionettes and dolls are found in many of the tourist shops, but these toys are substantially scarier than many children – or adults, come to that – can actually stomach. Wooden toys are also to be found in abundance, and the market at Havelska is particularly good for cheap toys that can keep small children amused for a while. Garnets are mined down the road in Teplice and are used in jewellery sold in almost every jeweller in Prague. The deep red stones are actually very attractive but are often set in over-elaborate surrounds and displayed in such abundance that they appear less appealing than they might otherwise.

Shopping in Prague has become far more cosmopolitan in recent years, with many of the top international fashion houses now making their presence felt in the city. British high-street stores such as M&S, Tesco and Mothercare have gained a foothold in the market, along with similar competition from the rest of Europe. You can find almost everything you need in the city, so you will no longer have to despair when you discover you've left your make-up or toothbrush at home.

The shops are not world class, but top-end international names are increasingly making their mark on the scene. If you look around Josefov, especially in Pařížská and U Prašné brány, you'll find some of the finest names. There are prices to match, but also some real bargains to be had. The Brioni shop, suit makers to Pierce Brosnan and Kofi Annan, will make a bespoke suit for just over £1,000 compared with about £2,750 in the UK.

Broadway Shopping Centre, Na Příkopě, P1.

A small shopping centre housing, among other things, the newspaper offices of DNES, but it's best used as a cut-through.

Dolce & Gabbana sells a lot of D&G clothing, but also stocks a range of other designers
Morgan French fashion for women with a slimmer figure. Sexy and stylish clothing.
Taiza a relatively new Prague fashion house hoping to make it internationally. With high-class designs using interesting materials, it boasts a full range of accessories to match. Good for evening wear.

Cerná Ruze, Na Příkopě, P1.

A three-storey shopping centre on this fashionable street, with a mix of Czech and international retailers. Housed in a beautiful old palace (of which only the original façade remains), it is one of the more attractive centres, although it's a pity about the signs.

Bang & Olufsen top-of-the-range audio equipment
Chevignon cowboys seem to be the order of the day
Moser Czech glass at its most ornate
Naf Naf French designer children's clothes to be found worldwide

Revlon in case you left your make-up at home, or fancy a little bit more

● **Jungmannova náměstí, P1.**

Lurking behind Wenceslas Square, this little square possesses a few decent shops:

Boss designer fashion with several stores across the city. Expensive for the Czechs, appealing to some.
Lancôme well set-out, fully stocked outlet for women who forgot to stock up at Duty Free
Sheron jewellery shop selling a variety of less tourist-orientated bits and pieces
Terranova smart, Italian high-street fashion for men and women spread over two floors

Koruna Palace, Václavské náměstí, P1.
www.koruna-palace.cz

A small Art Deco shopping centre on the edge of Wenceslas Square, Koruna has a pizzeria and bar as well as a selection of international shops at a discount price. The most interesting of these are:

Anima Tua raunchy women's wear from a range of small, individual designers
Bonton a large Czech music store – the equivalent of HMV – with its own popular radio station to boot
Bruno Magli famous Italian shoemaker, not as fashionable as elsewhere in Europe
Cesare Paciotti Italian footwear for men and women, but not as glamorous as it might sound
Swatch Swiss watch company with a range of practical and designer time-pieces
Timberland for the rugged city-dweller

Lucerna Passage, Vodickova, P1.

This passageway arcade concentrates primarily on photography and photographic equipment, with real estate coming in a close second. A handful of other shops, including a Levi's store and a handbag shop, make an appearance. Great if you want to buy a camera, new or antique. Look out for the horse hanging upside-down from the ceiling in one of the halls.

Melantrichova, P1.

Right in the centre, the main cut-through from Old Town Square to Wenceslas Square. Theoretically it should be full of high-quality shops, but instead tourist tack and the sex machine museum have taken over.

Art Decoratif Art Nouveau trinkets and antiques housed in a shop copied from Mucha's work in Paris
Biailo purveyors of designer outerwear. Prices are high but the quality is excellent.
Country Life If you can't live without lentils, pulses or Royal

Jelly for a couple of days, here is Prague's finest health food shop and café.

Goebal a large crystal shop, full of expensive glass, catering to an individual taste

Manufaktura makers of plain and simple, old-fashioned wooden toys. Great for children, and makes a welcome change from a Gameboy.

Myslbek, Na Příkopě, P1.

A large mall running off this busy shopping street houses an ample selection of international shops. Modern and very new, this could be anywhere in Europe.

Gant the all-American store that's achieved an all-action, yet undeniably clean cut and preppy look

Kookai French high-street fashion

Marlboro Classics American design for the understated cowboy. Stetsons optional.

Mothercare the ubiquitous British chain, selling a range of baby clothes and accessories

Sony the smarter end of the electronics scene

Tie Rack caters to homesick Brits and Czech anglophiles

Na Příkopě, P1.

A smart shopping street at the bottom end of Wenceslas Square, consisting of large shopping malls and chic individual shops. There are some decent jewellery shops, as well as the usual glass and tourist outlets. Halfway down is a helpful tourist information centre. Some of the more interesting shops include:

Adidas sportswear for the streets, but expensive by Czech standards. A mixture of classics and brand new apparel.
Benetton a flagship store, selling its ubiquitous collection of Euro fashion
Jackpot & Cottonfield Danish street wear: slightly smarter than usual, with clothes for women (Jackpot) and men (Cottonfield)
Lacoste classic French sportswear in a smart boutique, selling the latest range of products
Mango a Spanish clothes company, producing reasonably priced fashion and accessories for women, with stores across Europe
Marks & Spencer Yes, it gets everywhere; expect the same as your local high street with similar prices
Moser high-class glass, cut into a variety of shapes and forms, but not necessarily to everyone's taste since it tends to be overly ostentatious

Tango primarily a ladies' shoe shop with a mid-range selection of formal and casual shoes, which caters for men only minimally
Zara two storeys of reasonably priced Spanish fashion for men and women

Lined with designer shops and chic cafés, this is the smartest of all the shopping streets in the city – the equivalent of London's Sloane Street or Bond Street. If you have the money, this is the place to spend it. A variety of more expensive tourist shops has sprung up, selling a mix of antiques, crystal and jewellery.

Alberto Guardiani a shoe-maker displaying modernity and refinement, creating shoes for the young, chic and adventurous
Alfred Dunhill the quintessentially British store selling stylish fashion that has transcended time. Clothes are modern and fashionable, created with an unerring eye for style.
Escada Sport chic, casual clothes from an internationally renowned designer
Francesco Biasia home to some of the finest handbags in the city. Based on principles of natural simplicity, they are elegant, refined, stylish for all ages.
Hermes world-famous silk scarves, ties and accessories
Louis Vuitton luggage, leatherwear, handbags and fashion from a brand that is identifiable on every airport carousel
Le Patio one of a couple of lifestyle shops in the city selling antique and oriental furniture, wrought-iron candlesticks and stylish *objets* for the home.
Pringle Scottish-based design that has shed its golfing image for a more sought-after modern approach
Salvatore Ferragamo shoes, clothes and leather goods for

the sophisticated from this elegant Italian designer

Strenesse German style at a price; elegant clothing that will make you feel as glamorous as the natives

U Prašné brány, P1.

A little square behind the Municipal House, home to a selection of stylish boutiques that are typical of chic Josefov.

Beltissimo more leather and handbags in a sumptuous setting

Ermenegildo Zegna elegant menswear from the renowned Italian designer

Kenzo French fashion and perfume in a discreet little boutique

Leiser German shoes for men and women; not the most fashionable or elegant but full of Teutonic practicality

Mont Blanc pens, wallets and fashion accessories

Versace shopping heaven for the style-conscious and wealthy

Slovansky Dům, Na Příkopě, P1.
www.slovanskydum.cz

A smallish mall whose focus falls more on entertainment than shopping. Inside are three restaurants: a fantastic Italian, a conveyor-belt Japanese sushi bar and a lively Irish bar/restaurant. There is also a large 10-screen cinema showing all the latest films. The shops include:

Beltissimo supposedly high-class leather goods, shoes and handbags
Cerruti Jeans fashion based on natural and innovative fabrics
Escada Sport clothes for all occasions, business or leisure
Sparky's an offshoot of the most successful toy shop in the country

Wenceslas Square, Václavské náměstí, P1.

Wenceslas Square is the retail centre of Prague, where you will find the large department stores, neon signs and chain shops. The square was once a beautiful Art Nouveau space which over the last century has largely been destroyed by the emergence of modern stores. The shops hold nothing of much substance, but the better ones include:

Dum Mody five floors of Czech fashion. You've seen what the locals wear, so it's up to you.

Kenvelo an Eastern European equivalent of Gap, selling cheap, sporty clothing. More style than most and very practical.

Nike the flagship store in the Czech Republic with all the old favourites. It could be anywhere in the world.

Palac Kinh the 'Palace of Books': a large book shop over several floors, with a sizeable English language section, plus a good selection of international magazines

Promod women's fashion in a handsome, modern building on the corner, with some fun, different and sexy clothes

Železná, P1.

A small street leading from Old Town Square towards Wenceslas Square that's home to some small, designer boutiques. To be found here are:

Coccinelle high-fashion German handbags and shoes

Estéee Lauder make-up and beauty products from this renowned French house

Marina Rinaldi Italian designer producing sleek fashion for women

Sergio Rossi exclusive shoes for boys and girls, with handbags to match (for the girls!)

Stefanel Italian men's and women's wear, from this relatively young global company. Relaxed chic.

play...

There are alternatives to sightseeing! Why not spend some time soaking up the vibrancy of the city by watching a football match, an ice-hockey game or by going riding in the hills surrounding the city? Do something unusual that you might not do at home. Outdoor field sports enthusiasts can take the opportunity to hunt for wild boar, duck or driven pheasants. Adrenaline lovers have the opportunity to go kayaking, canoeing or maybe even sky diving. For the less actively inclined, why not drift over the countryside in a balloon or hire a small plane to check out the country's castles from the air? There are so many different ways to entertain oneself in Prague and its immediate surroundings.

The Czech Republic's two predominant sports are football and ice hockey, and 2004 proved a busy year for both of them. In the May the World Ice Hockey Championships were held in Prague, creating much excitement; tipped to win it the national team faltered before the final hurdle. While in June the national football team was in action at Euro 2004 and progressed to the semi-finals, unluckily going out to the eventual winners, Greece!. The Czechs prove to be formidable opposition at both, and it might be worth catching a Slavia or Sparta Prague match (both are fierce rivals in both disciplines).

In the summer hire a bicycle and ride around the streets and parks of the city, venturing further afield than you might otherwise, or play a found of golf in the verdant countryside. In winter, ice skating on frozen reservoirs can prove highly entertaining, especially with the help of grog from local stalls.

The Czech countryside is littered with therapeutic spas offering ranges of medicinal courses – relaxation spas are few and far between. Prague only has one of note and this has a distinctly Thai feel to it.

If you're feeling adventurous, try something from a range of activities that you might not have the opportunity to try at home. Remember, weekends away are not necessarily about museums and churches: change the emphasis, go kayaking or parachuting; do something you will never forget.

CYCLING

City Bike, Královorská 5, P1.
Tel: 077 618 0284 www.citybike.cz
Open: 10am–7pm daily

City Bike is one of the few places in the centre of the city where you can hire a bicycle for the day. Although cycle routes are not really demarcated in the centre itself, there are some good tracks leading out of the city, as well as some interesting parks where you can take a ride. Cycling is a fun way to see some of the city outskirts that you wouldn't visit otherwise. City Bike will give you some good tips on where to go, as well as supply you with maps and crash helmets.

FLYING

F-air, Benesov Airport, Bystrice.
Tel: 317 793 820 www.f-air.cz

Learn to fly or simply hire a plane (and a pilot) and take a flight around the beautiful bohemian countryside, flying low over elegant castles and traditional villages from 75kc per minute.

J.V. Ballooning, Prokpovo náměstí 9, P3.
Tel: 284 861 198 jvballooning@post.cz

Ride in a hot-air balloon over the countryside and the small market towns that typify the region. It's peaceful and slow, and a fantastic romantic option: organize a champagne breakfast surprise for your loved-one.

FOOTBALL

Football isn't the national game that it is in most European countries, even though the Czech team has been riding high in recent years; instead, the emphasis is on ice hockey. Domestic Czech teams rarely make it past the group stages of the Champions' League or the first couple of rounds of the UEFA cup, as most of their better players choose to play abroad in England, Germany and Italy. This means that the standard of some of the games might be lower than expected, but they can still be very entertaining on a Saturday afternoon.

CU Bohemians Praha, Vršovická 31, P10.

Tel: 274 771 806 www.fc-bohemians.cz

One of the smaller Prague teams: think Crystal Palace as opposed to Arsenal (Sparta). Popular more with ex-pats, they always seem to be on the brink of insolvency… and they're nicknamed the kangaroos. You'll have to ask them why.

FK Viktorka Žižkov, Seifertova, P3.

Tel: 222 712 503 www.viktorka.cz

A local Czech team that has a tiny following. Since it's reasonably close to the centre and has a friendly atmosphere, pop along to double the crowd. Tickets from 30kc.

SK Slavia Praha, Vladivostocká 2, P10.

Tel: 233 081 751 www.slavia.cz

SK Slavia Praha normally come second to Sparta, and theirs is the greatest rivalry. A favourite of the old republic and the more intellectual of the middle classes. A new stadium is in the offing.

Sparta Praha, Milady Horákové 98, P7.

Tel: 220 570 323 www.sparta.cz

The top team in the Czech Republic, although they have gone slightly downhill in recent years by European standards. They do provide some entertaining games in an impressive stadium, but the Premiership it's not. The evident skinhead element is worth avoiding – go for the more expensive seats. Tickets from 100kc.

GOLF

Golf is a relatively new sport in the country, hence good courses are few and far between. There is one 18-hole course near the centre of the city (see below), but there are other good courses surrounded by beautiful countryside. Contact the Tourist Information Centre for further details, and bear in mind that you'll need a car to reach them.

Erpet Golf Centrum, Strakonická 4, P5.
Tel: 257 321 177 www.erpet.cz/golfclub.html

In the centre of Prague is an indoor golf course, putting greens and a driving range, as well as swing simulators that allow you to play courses from around the world. Tennis, squash and swimming facilities are also to be found here.

Praha Karlštejn Golf Klub, Líten Běleč 280.
Tel: 0311 684 716 www.karlstejn-golf.cz
Open: 9am–7pm daily

A stunning 18-hole golf club located just outside the city. Set in beautiful countryside beneath the imposing castle, it is a joy to play. Green fees range from 1,000 to 1,800kc, so it might not be as cheap as you'd hoped.

HORSE-RACING

Velká Chuchle, Radotínská 69, P5.
Tel: 257 941 431 www.velka-chuchle.cz
Open: 8am–4pm on race days

This is the main race-course in the country and home to the Czech Derby as well as international races such as the Grand Prix of Czech Turf, Grand Prix of Prague and the President of the Republic's Prize, located in the south-western suburbs of the city and easily reached by taxi. Races are run every Sunday afternoon throughout the season (April to October), with a break in July. The bigger races are run in June and October and watching racing could be a different way to spend a Sunday afternoon.

HORSE-RIDING

The city centre is not a place to be on a horse, but there are some large parks in the suburbs and beautiful countryside outside the city. Rates are incredibly cheap (in comparison with London) and tuition is invariably offered.

JK Troja Praha, Pod Havránkou 7, P7.
Tel: 0602 376 455

Located in the northern suburbs, next to the zoo, JK Troja offers opportunities to ride in the hills that surround the city. You may bring your own horse if you just happen to have it with you! Follow up your ride with lunch at Svata Klara, a good Czech restaurant in an ornate cave.

Stáj Cinema Palace Hotel, Všenorská 45, Jíloviště.
Tel: 257 730 108

Forty kilometres from Prague, these stables nestle in the beautiful bohemian hills at the intersection of two rivers. The stables take care of everything, with staff speaking English, German and Russian. Prices for a whole day are roughly 2,000kc.

ICE HOCKEY

The national sport of the Czech Republic: ice-hockey fans are in fierce competition with neighbouring Slovakia. Most games are well attended, and can be quite ferocious at times. As with football, there are two main teams in Prague, Sparta and Slavia, who have an intense rivalry. The websites do tend to be in Czech, and are therefore quite tricky to decipher, but check local newspapers for dates of matches.

HC Slavia Praha, Vladivostocka 10, P 10.
Tel: 267 311 417 www.hc-slavia.cz

A smaller, more ramshackle stadium holding only 6,000. Slavia and Sparta derbies become very intense in the bear-pit atmosphere.

Sparta Praha, Za Elektrárnou 419, P7.
Tel: 233 378 229 www.hcsparta.cz

The wealthier of the two clubs but with a more working-class backing, Sparta now plays in the impressive T Mobile arena.

ICE-SKATING

Ice-skating is very popular in the Czech Republic; that figures, since ice hockey is the national sport. Ice rinks normally open for a couple of hours during the day in between hockey practices. In the winter, outdoor rinks open up in the centre (check the local papers for details). Skaters may also to be found on the reservoirs at Divoká Sárka and Hostivar in the winter months, and stalls selling alcohol can be found around the edge. Hire skates in town first.

HC Kobra, Mikuleckého 1441, Branik.
Tel: 241 490 132
Open: 1–3pm Saturday–Sunday only

An ice-hockey club that opens its doors at the weekend for people to come and play.

HC Praha, Na Rozdilu 1, Vokovicé.
Tel: 235 352 759 www.hc-hvezda.cz

Check the website or give them a call to find out exactly when the rinks are open (usually only at weekends, but it's worth checking first).

Sparta Praha, Za Elektrárnou 419, P7.
Tel: 233 378 229 www.hcsparta.cz

Home of the biggest ice-hockey team in the country. Check for times when it's open to the public.

Štvanice, Ostrov Štvanice, P7.
Tel: 233 378 327
Open: 7.30–10pm Friday; 1–3.30pm Saturday; 7.30–10am Sunday

Located on an island in the river this rink is part of a larger complex, which includes tennis courts in the summer.

KARTING

Go-Karts, Výpadová 1335, P5.
Tel: 602 343 580 www.kart-centrum.cz
Open: 3pm–midnight Monday–Friday; 11am–midnight
Saturday–Sunday

To the west of the city, this karting centre has both indoor and outdoor tracks. A small restaurant and bar help calm your nerves and sustain your adrenaline levels. It costs 200kc for 10 minutes and up to 2,000kc for 2 hours. The whole place is bookable by arrangement from 12,000kc an hour, and includes the restaurant.

Kart Klub, Hůlkova 16, P9.
Tel: 602 878 717 kleby@kartklub.cz
Open: 3pm–10pm Monday–Friday; 11am–10pm Saturday–Sunday

Cheaper than the others, with a bulk buy option of six karts for an hour at 5,200kc, so it's favoured by by stag parties. Presumably the Czech Republic's stringent drink driving laws don't apply on the track.

KAYAKING AND CANOEING

The country's numerous rivers and steep hills, make it ideal for this adventure sport. Take it to whatever level you wish: gently paddling down a flat stream or dropping off the edge of water-falls and shooting the rapids.

Aqua BM Sport, Na Heřbenkách 2, P5.
Tel: 257 215 439 www.vodackyraj.cz
Open: 10am–6pm daily

On the west bank of the Vltava, this sports store sells everything you need for kayaking at any level. It rents out canoes and can arrange for car-hire to transport them to the river. Prices start from 140kc a day for a kayak only.

Boatpark, Českomoravská 22, P9.
Tel: 266 035 875 www.boatpark.cz
Open: 8am–5pm daily

You can rent or buy canoes here at a slightly cheaper rate than at Aqua BM Sport above. They can deliver the boats to where you want to go at a rate of about 10kc per km and can advise on the best places to go.

PAINTBALL

Paintball Club Troja, Krejnická 2021, P4.
Tel: 272 762 938 www.paintballgame.cz
Open: 9.30am–6pm Monday–Friday only

The usual stag weekend activity, except this paintball shop bizarrely doesn't open on the weekend. There is equipment to buy or rent here and three distinct gaming zones to play in. Wear thick clothes, as it can get a little painful at times.

PARACHUTING

Aviatic Centrum Praha, Pujmanové 27, P4.
Tel: 261 226 450 www.clever.cz/~alarex/acp.htm

A chance to really cut loose; not a great romantic treat, but it may tickle your fancy. Learn to paraglide or parachute jump for 4,450kc, and it will be the ride of your life.

Tandem Centrum, Na pěkné vyhlídce 4, P6.
Tel: 233 343 443 www.pakady.cz

For 3,500kc you can do a tandem parachute jump with a qualified instructor; for an extra 1,000kc they will video the event. If you wish to fulfil a burning desire to leap out of a plane at 4,000ft without any clothes on, then this is your place – they'll even film that too.

SHOOTING AND HUNTING

Something different for a weekend away: try a day stalking deer and wild boar, or have them driven at you. There is always some element of risk involved, so it's not really recommended for those who have never handled a rifle or shotgun.

Interlov Praha, Jungmannova 25, P1.
Tel: 272 659 355 Info@interlov.cz

Interlov Praha organizes a range of hunting activities, including stalking roe, red, fallow and sika deer, chamois and wild boar. There are group hunts with driven wild boar shoots, as well as small game, including pheasant, wild duck and hare. Interlov provides all the necessary arrangements, including insurance and licences.

Shooting Gallery, Výstaviště 7, P7.
Tel: 220 103 620 www.zbraneak.cz
Open: 9am–9pm Monday–Friday; 10am–8pm Saturday–Sunday

Learn to shoot handguns at this shooting range in the suburbs of the city; you can live out some of those gangster fantasies by blowing away targets with a range of guns. No licence is required, and staff will provide instruction if it is your first time.

SPAS

Sabai, Slovanskě Dům, Na Prikope 22, P1.
Tel: 221 451 180 www.sabai.cz
Open: 10am–10pm daily

A new Thai spa in the centre of Prague. The prices are fantastic, with a range of therapeutic and relaxation massages starting at around 500kc for an hour. Traditional massages take place in this elegant little spa hidden above this busy shopping centre.

Hg2 Prague

info...

DANGERS

There is very little to be wary of in Prague. Violent crime in the centre and tourist areas is virtually unheard of, but there are, nevertheless, sneakier elements of the criminal fraternity who will try to rip you off. Pickpockets are one of them. They operate in crowded areas such as the Charles Bridge, and as people are getting on and off the underground, trams and buses, so be mindful of your valuables. The prostitutes around Wenceslas Square can be quite insistent, so don't be distracted by wandering hands – they won't just be groping you.

MONEY

The crown (CZK) is the unit of currency used in the Czech Republic. At the time of writing, the exchange rates are roughly: £1 = 48kc; $1 = 27kc; €1 = 32.

Gone are the days when you had to worry about bringing traveller's cheques or ordering wads of cash before you leave the UK. There are ATMs littered around Prague, the first of which are to be found at the airport. If you need larger sums of money, these can be withdrawn from local banks with the production of a passport. Try to avoid using a bureau de change, since you will inevitably get fewer crowns for your pounds, and never change money on the street – this is when you will be taken for a ride.

NEWSPAPERS

A good source of information for cinema, theatre and event listings is *The Prague Post*, which is published on a Wednesday and costs 50kc. It can be picked up from all good newsstands.

PUBLIC TRANSPORT

Public transport can be a little confusing. Tickets cannot be bought on buses or trams or even at some stops, but instead are purchased from underground stations and yellow machines on street corners, or can be bought from a café,

newsagent or tobacconist. Tickets have to be punched when you enter the underground, tram or bus in order to validate them, otherwise you may incur a 400kc fine if you're caught by an inspector (always ask to see their badge). A single ticket, valid for 15 minutes on any form of transport, is 8kc, an hour costs 12kc, 24 hours cost 70kc, while a weekend sets you back 200kc. Underground, bus and tram maps are available from newsstands, tourist information offices and underground stations. Visit www.dp-praha.cz for more details.

TAXIS

Taxis are notoriously unreliable in Prague – if you pick them up in the street they will try and rip you off. It is much better to call one of the local, reputable, English-speaking companies, who will pick you up from anywhere and not over-charge you. A taxi from the airport will charge you at a fixed rate (around 650kc), while a taxi to the airport should cost you between 300 and 400kc. Taxi drivers are legally obliged to use their meters, but it is often far simpler to negotiate a fare with the driver before you get in. Both AAA (tel: 14014) and Profi Taxi (tel: 14035) are reliable companies.

TELEPHONES

All the telephone numbers in this book are given without the international code but retain the city code prefix.

To call Prague from the UK, the international prefix is +420. The best way to phone while in the city is to use your mobile, so remember to have you international option activated. Phone cards, which you can buy from the local newsagent, tobacconist or at your hotel, are a better option than trying to find a coin-operated payphone.

TIPPING

In restaurants and cafés it is best to round up the bill or add a 5 or 10% tip (and about the same for a taxi ride). Do not be afraid not to tip if the service is shoddy or you feel that you have been ripped off.

index

index

index